THE INVITATION

22 church planters
from around the world
tell their stories

HOUSE
TO
HOUSE
PUBLICATIONS

House To House Publications
Lititz, Pennsylvania USA
www.h2hp.com

The Invitation

22 church planters from around the world tell their stories

Copyright © 2015 DOVE International

Published by House to House Publications
11 Toll Gate Road, Lititz, PA 17543 USA
Telephone: 800.848.5892
www.h2hp.com

ISBN 10: 0990429342
ISBN-13: 978-0-9904293-4-0

God is giving us an invitation
to join Him in planting
new churches to help people
come to faith in Jesus Christ.

CONTENTS

Introduction

I have heard it said hundreds of times: "We do not need more churches in our community. We have enough churches already."

I disagree. We cannot fulfill the Great Commission without planting churches. We need new churches! Jesus, when He ascended into heaven two thousand years ago, left a spiritual family of 120 believers in an upper room. That number multiplied into millions of believers who planted churches throughout the world. By planting new churches, we continue what Jesus started.

Here is another reason why we need new churches: A research study by Fuller Theological Seminary found that if a church is ten or more years old, only one person will be led to Christ for every 85 people in the congregation. If the church is between four and seven years old, one person is led to Christ for every seven members, but if a church is less than three years old, one person is led to Christ for every three members. That is why I agree with Dr. C. Peter Wagner, who often said that "the single most effective way to evangelize is to plant new churches."[1]

Here is yet another reason. The younger generations are leaving established churches by the hundreds. Many of them say they love Jesus but do not sense they are connecting with the local church. We cannot just write them off as being rebellious. At times, that may be the case; however, we cannot simply sit back and watch them leave. We must encourage each generation to start churches that will connect with their own generation. I am not saying that many of our young people will not continue to serve in our present local churches. They will and they should. But Jesus made it clear that new wine needs new wineskins (Matthew 9:17), and then both are preserved. The old and the new, serving right alongside one another!

Tim Keller, who pastors Redeemer Presbyterian Church in New York, writes and teaches extensively on the need for church planting. In his article, "Why Plant Churches," he writes, "The vigorous, continual planting of new congregations is the single most crucial strategy for 1) the numerical growth of the Body of Christ in any city, and 2) the continual corporate renewal and revival of the existing churches in a city. Nothing else—not crusades, outreach programs, para-church ministries, growing mega-churches, congregational consulting, nor church renewal processes—will have the consistent impact of dynamic, extensive church planting."[2]

He also writes that new churches best reach new generations, new residents and new people groups. Younger adults have always been disproportionately found in newer congregations.

New residents are almost always reached better by new congregations. In older congregations, it may require tenure of 10 years before you are allowed into places of leadership and influence, but in a new church, new residents tend to have equal power with long-time area residents.

Keller also suggests new socio-cultural groups in a community are always reached better by new congregations. . . . Brand new immigrant groups nearly always can only be reached by churches ministering in their own language. If we wait until a new group is assimilated into American culture enough to come to our church, we will wait for years without reaching out to them.

Every generation needs new churches (new wineskins) to connect with the next generations. That is why DOVE International began in 1980. At that time, my wife, LaVerne, and I loved Jesus and spent hours each day loving kids who hung out at our house. After a few years of trying to fit these young believers into the churches in our community and not being successful, the Lord opened our hearts to the possibility of starting something new. In 1980, we started a Sunday morning service with twenty-five people in a home in our community. Ten years later, the church had grown to include 2,300 people; now 300 churches in twenty nations.

People everywhere and of every age need Jesus. Age isn't the criterion. People of all ages may have difficulty relating to an established church for various reasons. Some people have had hurtful experiences, which hinder their ability to trust the leadership of the church. Some do not like structured services or the formality of it. Some people find it overwhelming to attend gatherings among a group of strangers. Many people find it difficult to build relationships with others within large congregations. Some people are simply unmotivated to get up Sunday mornings and attend church services. Whatever the reason, a large segment of the population is unchurched.

I believe that starting new communities of faith is one of our Lord's top priorities. He said, "I will build my church and the gates of hell will not prevail against it" (Matthew 16:18).

I am convinced that hundreds of believers will soon take a step of faith and plant new wineskins (new churches) to take care of the coming harvest. Other groups also have been answering God's call for church planting. Eight weeks ago I was in Stuttgart, Germany with a few hundred young German leaders from Hope International Ministries. A few years earlier, they had made a commitment to plant a new church within one-hour driving distance from every person living in the nation of Germany. Now—220 churches later—this vision has become a reality. Most of the 220 German churches are small vibrant churches with young leaders committed to reproducing more new churches. Most of the believers in these churches have come to faith in Christ within the past few years. These churches continue Jesus' vision to make disciples and fulfill his Great Commission (Matthew 28:19-21).

I am writing this chapter 35,000 feet above sea level on United Flight 492 returning to the USA from

Nairobi, Kenya. During the past few days, I have been inspired by my friends from Kenya, Uganda, Rwanda, Democratic Republic of the Congo and India who gathered for a DOVE leadership conference in Kitale, Kenya. I witnessed dozens of church leaders and future leaders make a commitment to plant at least one new church within the next year.

Why have they made this commitment? What does it really mean? Is it necessary? How will they fulfill their promise? Are they qualified? What do they need to do? How will these churches be different from established churches? What if they fail?

These are valid questions and deserve inspection. During the past years, many people have planted churches in the DOVE International family. The church planters grappled with the same questions. They faced difficulties and made some mistakes, but they persevered because they caught the vision of the Lord's heart for His Great Commission and Kingdom expansion. Some of the church plants are cell-based community churches, some are house churches or micro-churches, and others are large churches, but each has a story. I believe that reading the stories written by church planters is the best way for most questions to be answered. Their stories show how God uses ordinary people to fulfill His Great Commission in extraordinary ways. Let's get started.

—**Larry Kreider**

CHAPTER 1

Be obedient

Building effective churches in Brazil and Pennsylvania, USA

Chad and Chris Miller

You don't need to be someone special or a high achiever to plant a church—just obedient. Before my wife, Chris, and I married or even participated in any mission outreaches, we sensed God telling us, "Reach people where you are." So we did. I drove kids to youth functions and led a small youth cell group. I even met my wife through youth ministry.

After we were married one year, I had a dream. I saw a map of the world marked with red dots all over it, and sensed God saying, "You are going to touch these places in the world." When I awoke, the vision seemed so vivid. I protested, "God, I don't know any languages and I don't have a burning desire for any one nation. . . . What am I to do?"

Chris and I joined a team for a two-week mission trip to Brazil, where we both developed a concern for Brazil and a desire to help that nation. We enrolled in the DOVE Leadership and Ministry School, and later, in a language study school in Brazil. We asked God where we should live. Within that year, we moved to the city of Fortaleza, rented a home, and began teaching the Bible in the Portuguese language. We invited a Brazilian team of young adults from YWAM to work with us for ten days. During those days, we showed the Jesus movie, held numerous sports events and built relationships with kids and young adults. The relationships built during those ten days became our core group. Within a few weeks, we had fifty to seventy-five kids in our home daily. Almost all of the youth came from single-parent homes. We opened our doors at 9 a.m. for the kids to hang out and play games and sports. We closed the doors at noon for an hour. Chris and I did not have any children of our own, so that made it easier to open our home. At times the kids annoyed us, things got broken, but we became family.

We began a Sunday evening service and started a small group. Although the parents encouraged their kids to attend, they were not interested in pursuing God for themselves. Today the church is multi-generational, but it took about seven years before adults attended. Many of the youth who participated in our youth ministry are living for God today and did not become involved in drugs like family members and the kids around them did.

We learned that commitment fluctuates greatly when working with first-generation Christians. We had months of solid attendance followed by months of dwindling attendance. In fact, we saw the numbers fluctuating between six and sixty. That is very frustrating, but people need to see you will be there for them. Time builds trust.

We asked God how we could affect our community and open doors to them. The area was full of drugs and violence. We became proactive, praying in streets, serving at soup kitchens and bringing people into a safe environment. We saw miracles—including soup multiplying as we prayed because more people than we had expected showed up for a free meal.

We returned to the USA after seven years in Brazil. I became involved in youth ministry and serve as the youth leader for DOVE USA.

You don't need to be someone special or a high achiever—just obedient.

About two years ago, Chris and I planted a house church in Lititz, Pennsylvania. To plant an effective church, we must look at the need and meet it, not build a church around our need or what we want it to be. Chris and I saw that discipleship is the most important thing needed in our new house church called The Gathering.

Discipleship is knowing what the Word of God says and doing it. Discipleship doesn't normally happen during a preaching service. So we only have preaching every other week. On the alternate week, we break into discipleship groups. People can attend worship services and small groups every week and never be discipled or accountable to anyone. But having discipleship groups meet during the main service every other week, forces every person to be discipled. In these groups, we study the *Biblical Foundational Series*.[1] We apply what we are learning and share what God is doing in our lives. We pray and encourage each other.

We find by breaking into small groups and praying for each other, God touches people. We see the strength in discipleship. It's refreshing to see new Christians discovering with confidence that they are capable of discipling others.

The Gathering meets every Saturday night. People who are not connected with church come and accept Jesus. It's been surprising to see how The Gathering is growing into a multi-generational church. When Chris and I first started the church, we expected it to be made up of mostly young adults. But now we have lots of children, young and old, poor and rich, and multi-ethnicity. It doesn't matter the age or background, people desire community.

We want to create an environment that supports and allows transparency. People have a preconceived idea that church must be a certain way, but we believe that models and structures need to change if we are to reach people. Be real. People aren't looking for perfect leaders—but authentic leaders.

Another main goal for our group is church planting. We talk about church planting a lot. We meet with young adults to teach them that they can do more than lead a small group—they can plant a church. We find many young adults are ready and willing to plant a church. As leaders, we train and release them. If we wait too long, we get in a rut and never do it. Our goal is to plant more churches.

In Brazil, Chris and I planted a church by ourselves. Although that church plant was successful and continues to grow, we would not plant alone again. We believe it is important to have a team. Those who are interested in planting a church should meet with interested people and get a game plan.

Chris and I are called to plant churches, but we aren't going to recreate the same church over and over. Each church plant is different. One will become a micro church, another—a community church or mega church. The important thing is not structure, but whether discipleship is happening.

CHAPTER 2

Surprised by God

*Broadlands Community Church reaches out
in Virginia, USA*

Wallace and Linda Mitchell

It's astonishing that God called me to plant a church. I was not raised in a Christian home. In fact, I didn't even attend church until I was thirty years old.

My wife, Linda, and I had married right out of high school. Two years later while I was attending college, we had our son, Mitch. After college, I found myself in a devastating situation: no money, no car, no home. In desperation I cried out to God for help. Within two weeks I had a job, a car and a home. The first night in our new apartment, I tried to grasp how I had fallen into this good fortune. The only thing I could determine was that I had called out to God for help. I reasoned that if God could help me, I wanted to know who God was.

I went to the library to search for a book about God. Under God's guidance I found the book, *Archaeological History of the Jewish and Christian Faiths*, which routinely referenced the Bible. I decided I should read the Bible to find God. My wife had an old Bible that she had received while attending Sunday school as a little girl. I read through the entire Bible in about a year.

In Romans 3:23-25, I came to understand I was forgiven through Jesus Christ as I accepted Him as my Savior. At this point, I still had not attended a church. I worked for the government and was transferred to Washington, D.C., where we had our daughter, Nicole. Although life became more financially stable for us, Linda and I had deep marriage difficulties and separated for two and one-half years.

During that time I started attending a Bible church, which gave me much needed discipleship and ultimately helped restore our marriage. Eventually I became an elder in that church and later an associate pastor. Through that church, I attended a cell group conference where Larry Kreider was speaking. His teaching opened up the world of "cell church" to me, and began to answer questions I had about the spiritual gifts described in 1 Corinthians 12:7-11. With this enlightening at the age of 50, the Lord stirred in my heart to plant a church in another county. I shared my desire with the pastor and elders who prayed with me, questioned me and encouraged me to put in writing my desired purpose, vision, values, organization, administration and leadership structure. This was very helpful because it provided documentation for the foundation on which we eventually built the church.

Although the whole cell church concept was different from the practices of my church, the leaders approved the church plant and agreed to pay my full salary and all church planting expenses for one year. The leaders allowed me to present the proposal to the congregation and release anyone who wanted to come with me.

For six months, the church plant met in the existing church's youth room during the same time as the Sunday morning service. At the end of that time, we

Because we focus on small groups, people are ministered to in a variety of ways. We have developed a strong family atmosphere.

moved into a school located in the area where the church would be planted. In six years, due to the support of our releasing church, the faithful giving of our members and a miracle of God, we were able to buy five acres of land in the center of a densely populated residential area. We were able to build phase one of a two-phased building project. In growing the church, I applied the principles I learned from DOVE International. I think I may have been one of the first persons to complete the DOVE Leadership and Ministry School.

Our philosophy changed from traditional to cell church. Another change included embracing the gifts of the Holy Spirit. Having the blessing of our sending church and the insight from DOVE International was the greatest blessing for the planting of Broadlands Community Church. This above everything else contributed to our survival and ministry.

Despite this great start, I failed to see the importance of continual association, networking and training with those in a church planting movement. Our former church released us to chart our own course. Due to philosophical and vision differences, I did not turn to them to deal with the issues that surfaced in starting a church. In the beginning, while absorbing what DOVE International had to offer, attending many conferences and training sessions, I did not follow through with the DOVE connection. This hindered my leadership and our growth and ministry. After ten years, I felt isolated and saw the need for more relationship, support and accountability with likeminded brothers and sisters. I called Larry and asked to meet with him. He was very gracious and helpful. Soon we began the engagement process and now we are very happy to be a partner church with DOVE International.

We are committed to small groups, which form the core of our entire ministry. From the very beginning, we incorporated discipleship into our small groups. This has worked well and people have blossomed and matured in this family atmosphere. We offer book studies and Bible studies in our small groups. Because we focus on small groups, people are ministered to in a variety of ways. We have developed a strong family atmosphere. We encourage our groups to be creative on their outreaches. Every other month one group will sponsor its individual creative outreach, which other groups will be invited to participate. We use the term easy/easy for these outreaches. Meaning the event is easy to ask people to attend (non-threatening) and easy for people to come (non-threatening) with the purpose of building relationship. This has worked well and is enjoyable.

A lesson I learned from experience is that I attempted to make the groups and events too structured for everyone. You might say I was so ideologically committed to cell groups that I missed the principle of family and relationship. We leave each event to the discretion and creativity of the group, and this variety of approaches works well. Basically people meet people based on who they are and their shared unique interests. We also have several church-wide events, which are meant totally to enhance cell group participation. Some of these are Christmas Eve service, Easter Egg Hunt, and Vacation Bible School. Everyone seems to enjoy the church-wide involvement and looks forward to asking their friends to attend. Again, the idea is to build relationships with those without a church home.

My teaching gift worked well in discipleship but not so well in outreach. I taught on outreach more than I participated in outreach. Now I am more conscious of modeling personal evangelism. I also personally facilitate an Alpha course for non-believers, which fits nicely into the cell group vision and encourages outreach and participation in small groups.

Today, we at Broadlands Community Church are still learning and still excited about what God has in store. We believe a great move of God is unfolding and we are in a position to participate. God is faithful!

CHAPTER 3

Tricked into becoming church planters

in Massachusetts, USA

Lee and Teresa DeMatos

Teresa's story:

God tricked us into becoming church planters. When you read our story, I think you'll understand why we say we were tricked. Lee and I had been married five challenging years, raising three wonderful children—mine, his and ours. Our marriage was a mess. One day my estranged father invited me to attend a family reunion where I met Uncle Dan for the first time. He asked me two questions: "Do you know Jesus? Do you put Him first in your life—before your husband and your kids?"

Those questions haunted me. About a month later, my marriage exploded. This was my second marriage to fail. I screamed at God about marriage and how it doesn't work. When I stopped yelling, all I could hear echoing in my mind were those two questions Uncle Dan had asked: "Do you know Jesus? Do you put Him first in your life?"

I was ready to surrender and prayed, "Lord, I do want to know you, and I will put you first."

Immediately peace and hope entered my heart. Surprisingly, Uncle Dan called and asked, "Why are you on my mind?" I answered, "I'm going through a crisis in my marriage, and I just surrendered my heart to Jesus." Uncle Dan drove from Alabama to Massachusetts to see us and led Lee in a prayer of salvation. Believe me, Lee was ready. He said he saw the change in my life and wanted what I had.

Two years later we attended our first DOVE church, Lighthouse Christian Center, and knew we were home. Later, we traveled a bit but remained with DOVE churches. Some were house churches, some large churches, one was a youth church held in a garage.

"I'll flip them up on the dock and you clean them up," I said. But Pastor Joe said, "Nope. God is moving in your neighborhood, run with it. . . ."

When we came to Worcester, Massachusetts, we attended Calvary Worship Center and helped with a DOVE youth church on Tuesday nights. I taught children's church, and Lee formed a worship team. Through serving with Calvary Worship Center, we learned valuable principles of church planting, but we had no intentions to plant a church.

We live on an island on a small lake in Worcester. Living on the water was a dream for us . . . so right away, Lee asked God if he could buy a boat. The Lord said, "No, I want you to ask the neighbors to take you skiing instead."

That was a great way to connect with people. You see, we had prayed for opportunities to meet and build relationships with our neighbors. Lee loves water skiing, 4-wheeling, snowmobiling and construction work. Our neighborhood is full of guys who love those activities, so building relationships was easy for him.

I stayed home and prayed—and that brought results. A neighbor invited us to a Christmas party that conflicted with our church Christmas party. We prayed and asked the Lord what to do. We went to the neighborhood party where Jesus opened the door for us to share our testimony. A woman was deeply touched and shared her struggle with depression and suicide. We asked if we could pray for her. Two weeks later, God answered exactly as we had prayed! That same year, we had a terrible ice storm that left our island without power for six days and gave us the opportunity to share our generator with our neighbors and build relationships. These are a few examples of how we live out Christianity in our everyday lives.

Lee is the evangelist, and I am the prayer warrior. The Lord led me to pray and fast during the month of March that first year we lived on the island. All that I heard from God were the words: "It's time to march!" We obeyed, not knowing specifically what was coming.

That first summer, the Lord moved like lightning! The lady from the Christmas party got saved and other neighbors too! We started a Bible study August 12, 2009 with five people. Soon thirty-five people attended. By October, we didn't fit into any living rooms on the island. At that time, multiplying the group was not possible because the attendees were all new believers. We kept inviting all of our neighbors to church on Sundays. November 2009, Pastor Joe Ford told Lee to go and get a building. Lee said, "I don't want a building. You have a great building. I'll flip them up on the dock and you clean them."

But Joe said, "Nope. God is moving in your neighborhood, run with it. . . ." That is how God tricked us into becoming church planters.

Lee's turn:

As I walked around the island, the Lord spoke to me about a carpet of prayer. We discovered that many Christians before us (for fifteen years earlier) had prayer walked through our neighborhood. We received the harvest from those that went before us. The Lord led me to lay hands on the local bar in our neighborhood while the home group prayed. I laid hands on it and claimed it for the Kingdom of God in Jesus' name! The bar closed in six weeks! YAHOO JESUS!

We prayed for another month before asking the landlord if we could start a church in the building of the former bar. He said, "yes" and even dropped the rental price by thirty percent. For forty years, the bar had been known for drug dealing, prostitution and even murder. Demons were all over that place, but the body of Christ surrounded us and helped us clean the place.

On March 3, 2010, we held our first worship service in the former bar. It was the anniversary of the murder of the brother of one of the guys who I led to the Lord. He prayed the dedication prayer, "LORD I dedicate this place that the devil used for evil. You will restore it for good." We all cried and shouted victoriously! God certainly answered that dedication prayer. During that service and ones to follow, many lost people came to receive Jesus: drunkards, drug addicts, prostitutes, strippers, bullies. . . .

People have been physically healed, delivered from drug and alcohol abuse, marriages restored, broken families made whole and disciples made. We are so humbled by how God uses us. We continue growing. We meet in home groups during the week and hold two services Sunday morning. We're looking for a bigger building! Thank You, Jesus! HE truly gets all the credit.

CHAPTER 4

Look what God has done in Kenya

Ibrahim and Diane Omondi

When we held our first cell group in our home, we never envisioned that DOVE Africa would grow to about 200 congregations that reach into Kenya, Uganda, Rwanda and the Congo. By God's grace, the church in Africa continues to grow as new congregations are added to our numbers every year.

In the beginning, getting to know neighbors in Nairobi was not easy; most people live life behind large gates or locked doors. But our little boys, aged 2 and 3 years at the time, had become friends with some neighbor children in the large field behind our house. That gave me a "right" to knock on the doors of their parents, and introduce myself as "Mama Michael" (Michael's mom). We invited a few neighbors to a small group Bible study, and from there, DOVE was born.

In 1988, our living room hosted this first cell group. The members were churched—but not-yet-saved—neighbors who were open to hearing more about the Word of God. We met once a week to study the Bible, pray for each other and share a cup of tea.

We tried diligently to follow up on those who attended by visiting them in their homes. That worked for two or three of the families, but a majority of them found polite ways to become too busy to even entertain our attempts to "reach" them.

After several months of meetings, with attendance wavering depending on the week, one of the ladies gave her life to Christ—a significant breakthrough. She immediately became a fervent evangelist. She invited her family members, her friends and her workmates to the cell group. Before long, our home was too small. We started a second, and then a third cell group, in nearby neighborhoods.

"Is this a church?" we were often asked in those early days. "Yes, we have a vision to become a church," we always answered. We did not want to be accused later on of deceiving people or tricking them to be involved in something that was different from what was expected. Some of the first cell group participants were actually members of other churches, so we wanted to let them know what we were up to.

About one year later, we were asked to take another step. Those who had been attending felt that if we really wanted to be a church, we should start Sunday morning meetings. So we did. In a rented office space about two miles from our home, we had our first Sunday church service in 1989. Twenty-two people were present. We even had a Sunday school class for children and took an offering, which we had never done in the home cell group.

After another six months, the office was too small. We started meeting in a nearby school, and continued there until 2008 when DOVE acquired property in Nairobi and put up a tent as a place of meeting.

How did planting 200 congregations in Kenya, Uganda, Rwanda and the Congo happen? God orchestrated it in several different ways. From our midst, we started sending out church planters. Most of them have moved on to plant not only one church but to spearhead a church planting movement of their own.

Even if we had tried, we could not have planned the amazing growth in DOVE Africa. God is sovereign and is using His people—in His own way—to expand the Kingdom.

Yes, many times it felt difficult to send out our "best." But God the Father sent His one and only Son. Certainly we never have a right to complain. Even if we had tried, we could not have planned the amazing growth in DOVE Africa. God is sovereign and is using His people—in His own way—to expand the Kingdom.

We made an abundance of mistakes along the way. Looking back, we see the most obvious ones:

- assuming that friends whom we had ministered with and known for many years were the ones with whom to build the church;

- assuming that those same friends would recognize Ibrahim as the spiritual leader of the movement and honor that leadership;

- sending out church planters too soon, before they had fully been immersed in the DOVE vision, values and methods;

- adopting churches or leaders who "said" the right things but really did not understand the vision and mission of DOVE;

- giving the impression, albeit unintentionally, that DOVE in Africa is funded by and administered from the DOVE church family in the developed world.

Our desire is not only to see new nations coming into the DOVE family of churches, but also to raise healthy leaders and healthy congregations. Together with the DOVE family around the world, we believe that our church family will grow to one thousand congregations by the year 2020. How will this happen?

The DOVE Kampala leadership team is already working on a strategy that will be adopted and carried out over Uganda. Kenya leaders will encourage regional strategies towards this goal. DOVE Nairobi, which has recently been training Great Commission evangelists with Kenya's branch of Campus Crusade, will soon release some of those evangelists into church planting venues. We have identified three areas that could yield new congregations by mid-2015.

DOVE Africa is active in developing a strategy for raising church planters through leadership training and schools of evangelism. We want to identify

new fields for church planting and carry out satura-
tion prayer and evangelism in the identified areas.

We believe that the time is now for DOVE Africa
pastors and evangelists to reach out into the harvest fields, bring in the harvest and release men and
women of God, young and old alike, to plant new
churches.

CHAPTER 5

From house to house
in a multi-ethnic vibrant city

Church planting in Pennsylvania, USA

Craig and Tracie Nanna

Our story is more about stepping out in faith than a step-by-step text book on "this is how you should plant a church." The church planting vision was sown in our hearts during college when a group of friends gathered to pray and talk about church planting in the northeast United States.

Immediately after college, I accepted an associate pastor position in my hometown in western Pennsylvania. Four years later, my wife, Tracie, and I received a call to serve on the mission field in Peru. During our training for Peru, I had a vision of a church plant in an ethnically diverse city somewhere in northeast U.S. Because we were on our way to Peru for what we thought would be three years, we tucked this in our spirit as a prayer assignment. Little did we know that our time in Peru would only last six months.

We knew we had a call from God for ministry and did not quite understand the turn of events. With two toddler boys and another child on the way, we returned to the States. In desperation, I set my heart to hear from God. During those days of prayer and fasting in a tent on my grandparents' farm, it became clear that the vision I had during our missions training was for now.

My cousin just happened to be visiting the farm during that same time and mentioned Reading, which is an ethnically diverse city of great need in eastern Pennsylvania. After a few prayer journeys to visit Reading and some major confirmations (like a house for our family), we took the leap of faith and moved to Reading. Our home church in western Pennsylvania did not have vision to send us out as church planters, but we knew we had to obey God and trusted Him to bring us under authority with those of like vision.

We had a vision to plant a cell-based church, but not having any connections, we started by renting a neutral space in a local fire hall to begin an evangelistic small group. Very quickly we found a more suitable outreach location using the aerobics room of the local health and fitness club. We had favor with the owners. The owner's wife eventually became a Christian and they allowed us to advertise on their doors and walls. We read a church planting manual that advised doing a mass mailing in the surrounding community. We also hung up flyers in nearby public places. One person came as a result of the mass mailing. However, that one person introduced us to her family members, and God began to do a work in each one of them. In the early days of building, we saw the Holy Spirit do that often. He is still doing that today—divine connections, word of mouth—people whose lives are being changed are now bringing their family and friends, and, as a result, households are being saved!

The first years of the church plant were definitely challenging and required great sacrifice, especially financially. At first, I thought we could be fully supported missionaries to Reading, but our international support seemed to dry up, except for a few faithful people who continued to partner with us in prayer and finances. But God had other plans. His provision was through a full-time job in a social agency that took me into homes, schools and streets of Reading. Soon, this city where we knew no one, became "our city" with real faces, real brokenness and real opportunity for the Gospel.

We also saw the clear hand of the Lord helping us in that first year with a divine connection with DOVE International. We were not alone anymore—we now had a spiritual family with the same heart and the same vision for advancing the Kingdom of God through church planting. Through DOVE's oversight and relationship, we soon met a group of believers in the Reading area who were traveling to the next town for church, but were praying for a church plant in Reading. This small group of believers became a vital part of our new church plant, and some became our first leadership team. Most church planting manuals necessitate having a church planting team when you launch. My wife and I did not have that—we were the team with our three kids! But God heard our cry and gave us a team that was already waiting for us here in Reading.

After a year, we had the team in place to begin to meet for corporate worship. We began to meet in homes during the week. The church was planted and the vision was coming to pass. Through much prayer, spiritual warfare and team growth, we are now, by the grace of God and for His glory, a multi-ethnic vibrant church, transforming Reading house to house!

CHAPTER 6

Why I love planting churches

70 churches planted in Uganda

Ephraim and Jova Tumusiime

Although my parents were born-again pastors in a Ugandan Anglican church, I believed while growing up that salvation was only for adults. At age 28, I was already married and had children when I was invited to visit a friend's church and ultimately became a disciple of Jesus.

Our pastor encouraged our small, young fellowship to grow by reaching out to the lost. I learned that I am under the Lord's command to "go" and "make disciples." This is a mandate that I realized I have no choice but to obey. This compelled me to prepare for Christian ministry. In 1991, I joined Daystar University College in Nairobi, Kenya, where I quickly became a member of DOVE Nairobi. The warmth I felt in DOVE Nairobi through the relationships I developed with members, encouraged me to participate in the whole life of the church. When I graduated, the elders challenged me to go back to my country and start a DOVE church.

It is exciting to see the lost getting found and becoming believers. It is within the fellowship that the new believers get discipled. As they get transformed into Christ-likeness and serve, the joy of ministry becomes unequalled as we see the recent enemies of the cross defending it! That is why I like starting churches—and have planted about seventy churches.

While studying in Nairobi, I had been particularly excited by the relationships built in the church through cell groups; I desired to see this happen in my homeland in Uganda. So when I moved back to Kampala, Uganda, my wife, Jova, and I started a new church in our home. We met on our porch and hung up a tarp to keep us dry when it rained. I learned that I should pray that the Lord would bring people that would become part of the outreach. The Lord indeed brought people, many of whom I had never met before.

It is exciting to see the lost getting found and becoming believers. As they get transformed into Christ-likeness and serve, the joy of ministry becomes unequalled as we see the recent enemies of the cross defending it!

In the beginning, I was quick to choose leaders and I made some mistakes. I gave titles to some leaders that I felt were going to work with me in reaching out to the lost. These titles were unbiblical. One fellow that I chose to be our church chairman started assuming powers like those of worldly organizations and that started hurting our ministry.

When we abolished the position, he left our ministry with negative words against us. Since then, I have learned to identify people's gifts and understand their commitment to our vision before placing them on a leadership team.

Discipleship has been incorporated into our cell groups, but often with great difficulty. Many of our cell groups are made up of members that are illiterate. We disciple these people with a lot of patience and love. The youth have been easier to disciple because the majority of them are literate. They seem to be more available and teachable than the adults, and, therefore, their cells are more actively involved in discipleship. Their cells easily multiply as they build relationships with other young people. The former young people in our church, from five to ten years ago, are now the members in our couples' cells in our church! This is very exciting to me!

Recently, exciting work began among South Sudanese refugees in northern Uganda. A typical example of how we begin new church plants is how we planted a church at Rhino Camp Refugee Settlement in the Arua District. Live music, dancing and the sound of a ram's horn enticed refugees to gather from different parts of the refugee camp to hear the Word of the Lord. A young refugee from the Congo preached powerfully in the English language. Because the majority of the refugees are from South Sudan, the message was translated into Arabic. During the altar call, more than eighty people gave their lives to Christ!

DOVE Uganda has also started four Early Child-hood Development Centers (ECDCs) within the four refugee clusters of Rhino Camp. The four clusters house more than 15,000 refugees. Each ECDC has about 250 hungry children. The refugees are very needy and it requires a lot of funds to pay teachers, provide meals for children and comply with the government's requirement for us to provide pit latrines, playgrounds with play materials, and proper structure for learning with seats and fenced learning areas.

We are building kingdom relationships with the refugees. When peace returns to northeastern Democratic Republic of the Congo and the Republic of South Sudan, the refugees will return home, and DOVE will have bases from which Bible-believing congregations will be planted. Such church planting vision excites me. That's why I love planting churches!

CHAPTER 7

Answering God's call is key for Kenya

God transforms desires, lives and a village

Hesbone and Violet Odindo

I know what it is like to depend on the Lord alone. Growing up in an alcoholic family in Kenya, I surrendered my life to God when a high school teacher invited me to a Christian weekend challenge. From that moment on, I started praying and fasting for my parents and nine siblings.

After high school graduation, I worked as a school teacher and participated in an evangelism team that preached the Gospel in many different areas. One day, the team ministered in my home village, and both my parents and my brother received Jesus as Lord and Savior.

Doors soon opened for me to study in India. On the flight to India, I cried out to God, "Oh, Lord, You have put a poor village boy in your plan. If you keep me safe and make my studies successful, I will serve you for the rest of my life."

While studying for a Bachelor of Commerce degree, I led an international students' fellowship in North India and, with other students, founded a fellowship in Punjab University and planted four other congregations.

One evening while traveling on a bus to a crusade, the Lord spoke to me. "I have called you to go serve my people."

God's call did not bring me comfort, because my plan was to work and make a lot of money to support other ministers. I prayed, 'Lord, please give me ten years to work, build a house for my mom and myself and buy a car, then I will serve you full-time.'"

God was very patient with me. The more I fasted and prayed, the clearer the call unfolded. When the time came to return to my home country, I prayed the Lord would lead me to a church that would use my gifts to extend the kingdom. God did.

In June 1993, I felt a confirmation in my spirit when I visited a Sunday celebration at DOVE Nairobi. I became part of a vibrant youth fellowship where I met the love of my life, Violet. We married in 1995 and started a cell group in our home. I was appointed an elder and later became an associate pastor under the leadership of Ibrahim and Diane Omondi.

Although busy combining ministry with a career in hospital administration, I did not forget God's call to full-time ministry. Neither could I forget my village, Kadawa, which was being ravished by disease.

More than 40 percent of the villagers had HIV/Aids. In 2005, a medical team visited my village. One of the leaders said, "If nothing is done, this village will be wiped out within ten years."

I knew only a holistic ministry could save my people. In 2006, I attended the DOVE International Leadership Conference. The theme that year was "Occupy and Expand." On the last day of the conference, the Lord instructed me to start a cell group in the Kadawa Village where I grew up. I started a cell church in my mother's home. Seven months later, thirty people were members and agreed to help start a Sunday service. My wife and I moved to the village to be in full-time ministry. Our departure was not easy because we had bonded so well with our spiritual parents. It was made even harder because we did not receive monetary support from DOVE Nairobi. However, that turned out to be good. It made us dependent on the Lord who is Jehovah Jireh.

The first service was held in 2007. Today, two services are held in the original church building every Sunday, and seven more congregations have been planted. That numbers about 2,000 who love Jesus. The Lord is delivering many from darkness, immorality, drug addiction and witchcraft. As people are taught hygiene, it has helped stop cholera. HIV/Aids and other infections are declining due to changes in behavior. Malaria cases have been reduced through mosquito bed net distributions and by removing bushes around houses. The latest demographic shows life expectancy has improved from 37-40 years to 45-60 years. Ignorance is being reduced as parents enroll their children in school. Twenty-eight female and three male orphans are attending a boarding school due to divine partnerships. Destitute widows are being cared for; wetlands that were not producing food are now productive farm lands. In addition, neighboring churches are being transformed through hearing what God is doing. The transformation of Kadawa would not have happened without the prayer and financial resources of the DOVE family and other divine partnerships.

We trust the Lord to plant fifty celebrations by 2020, and to build Victory Christian School to give students from kindergarten through high school an excellent education. In addition to traditional school curriculum, we plan to add trade courses such as business training, carpentry, electricity, dressmaking, tailoring and information technology.

Let us remember the past is history, the future is a mystery, today is a gift. What we do with the gift the Lord has given us is crucial for church expansion.

CHAPTER 8

Planting churches in Cape Town, South Africa

Cheree and Merle Shenk

Cheree and I, with our 9-month-old daughter, moved from the USA to Cape Town in 2004 to plant a church. Although we had helped plant churches in other areas of the world, we were unprepared for the steep learning curve we faced in the developing nation of South Africa.

We had difficulty making personal contact with people. Frustrated, I started conversing with the security personnel at the development complex where we lived. One man was having marriage trouble. I prayed with him and shared some impressions that I sensed God showed me. A few days later, the man ran up to tell me that his wife had come back just like I had prayed.

"I am waiting for you to start a church so that I can come," he said.

I asked, "Are you willing to have us come to your house and start a prayer meeting"? Our first small group started in a cramped apartment where four families were living in what was one of the roughest areas of inner city Cape Town.

We experienced God doing amazing things! We saw major answers to prayer! From that first house group, the church was birthed. We moved to a public hall when the apartment could no longer hold us. From there we launched seven cell groups.

About eighty people attend the church and we are planting a new church in Athlone. We have started a Bible school called Jeremiah Training Center and REACH School of Supernatural Ministry, which focuses on training believers in supernatural outreach and planting small groups that potentially become churches. We have seen God open amazing ministry opportunities as we reach out and He heals people who have been deaf and blind, those who have been in car accidents or suffer from pain and sickness.

Frustrated, I started conversing with the security personnel at the development complex where we lived. One man was having marriage trouble. I prayed with him and shared some impressions that I sensed God showed me. A few days later, the man saw me and ran up to tell me that his wife had come back just like I had prayed.

Although we have made many mistakes, I will share some of those that turned into helpful learning experiences for us.

1. As a western missionary in a developing nation, people deferred leadership to us almost automatically. Allowing this was a huge mistake. At one point I was personally leading seven small

group meetings a week. It fulfilled my need as a missionary to do something but stifled multiplication and growth. When the responsibility became too much for me, I handed over the leadership of each small group to those in the group. Not one of those small groups existed six months later! With some exceptions, we have found that gathering in small groups must be the initiative of those who will lead them long term. We now mentor those with this initiative.

2. We made the mistake of trusting gifted people who had not led small groups. We thought if we treated people like leaders they would rise to that standard. They didn't. It actually had the adverse affect of concreting their current character weaknesses instead of encouraging character growth. This caused a lot of pain to us, to them and to others.

3. Our knee-jerk reaction to mistake number 2 caused us to swing from one side of the pendulum to the other. We made a requirement for potential leaders to fulfill two years of ministry training before they could become department heads or elders. Although we deeply believe in the value of theological training, we found that people who committed to this level of training seemed more interested in being good students than good leaders in the local church. Again, their character wasn't being developed, and they were getting head knowledge but not experience.

Leading small groups is a good way to verify a potential leader. We have seen God build character in those who are gifted and knowledgeable. We have also seen Him developing the gifting and knowledge of those who don't feel they could ever be leaders. We have learned to not promote someone beyond where God has developed his or her character. Our current process is intentionally training potential leaders and mentoring them through the challenges of their own life, as God builds their character, while having them start and/or lead small groups.

4. Pouring hours and hours into people who did not pour life into other people was a huge emotional drain, as well as wasting time and energy. We have learned to invest our energy into people who are sons of peace, described by Jesus in Luke 10:6. Sons of peace are open (willing to talk to us about spiritual things), hungry (wanting to learn more of God) and sharing (willing to share in his circle of influence what God has done). In the REACH School of Supernatural Outreach and Ministry, we teach those principles in depth. In the beginning, I confused those people wanting to tell me their problems with those who were actually hungry. Many times problems can make people hungry enough to change their ways, but our experience is that it is not until they are truly sick and tired of the way things are that they are truly hungry to follow God's Word.

5. Another mistake is assuming that teaching biblical knowledge and principles is the same as discipling people. Merely teaching discipleship courses allows people to become inactive Christians. Now our discipleship programs focus on the central theme of obedience to the commands of Christ. Our small groups emphasize practical goal setting and how to practically and measurably obey Christ's commands every week. This emphasis has resulted in God doing more ministry through more people than in previous years of us "working hard."

We excitedly look forward to see more churches planted through disciple making movements and to train and help others do the same.

CHAPTER 9

Not Pottstown!

Replacing our dreams with God's purposes in Pennsylvania, USA

Todd and Jessi Clemmer

One evening while driving home from the DOVE Leadership and Ministry School, my husband Todd said, "Maybe we might actually plant a church someday. I kind of feel like, maybe in Pottstown."

"Pottstown!" I exploded. "I don't even like Pottstown! If God wants me to move to Pottstown and plant a church, He'll have to kill me and start over!"

As it turns out, God did have to "kill" some parts of me, the ones that were solely my flesh and needed to go in order for Him to bring new life. We now live in Pottstown. This year was the ninth anniversary of Koinonia House, the church we planted in Pottstown.

Todd and I had known early on in our marriage that we were called to ministry. Over the years, we served as youth leaders, led various Bible studies and even led a marriage ministry. In 1999, the clear call to church leadership was confirmed by our pastor, elders and mentors. But how? Did it mean schooling? Full time pastoring? What would be my role in ministry (as the church we were part of did not include women on the eldership team)?

We had more questions than answers, but we did have a definite sense that God was prompting us to press forward in seeking Him for direction. About this time, a friend shared a message that he had heard from a guest speaker named Larry Kreider. The theme of the message was "approaching the point of no return." Larry used the analogy of an airplane on a runway, moving ahead and picking up speed, and eventually reaching a critical point where it must either take off or crash.

Both Todd and I sensed this analogy meant that we were to act on something. As a result of hearing Larry's message, we checked out DOVE and found out about the DOVE Church Planting and Leadership School (now called the DOVE Leadership and Ministry School). Within a matter of weeks, and through a series of God-planned events, Todd enrolled. Since we had two small children and one on the way, I did not enroll but sat in to audit classes whenever my schedule allowed.

Initially our mindset was not at all to plant a church. Todd and I felt that we were attending the school more for the "leadership" part. We envisioned remaining comfortably in our local church where we had been for many years, and maybe taking on more responsibility there. We loved the people in our church family and were in no way looking to "jump ship," which made Todd's comment about church planting in Pottstown all the more shocking to me.

After Todd finished the classes at the DOVE school, we continued for a few more years of involvement with our church. At the same time, we were maintaining and growing connections within DOVE. Our sense of leadership not only grew, but also our clarity on what ministry could look like for us became clearer. We learned the importance of cell groups. All the while, we continued to share openly with the leaders at our church.

Eventually, we sensed that God was directing us to start something new. Our home congregation, our personal friends and mentors and DOVE leaders agreed and voiced confirmation. We were entirely blessed to have the affirmation of our current church leaders, who expressed that support not only to us but also publicly to the congregation. They even encouraged people who

We've had to learn to stop looking at others to gauge if we are doing well. Constantly we need to remember to look to Him alone for the "well done." Sometimes the things we want to do aren't actually the things He is asking us to do.

might be interested in joining us in this new venture to begin meeting with us for prayer on a weekly basis. For about six months, we had a small group of people gathering in our home for what started as a prayer meeting and later emerged as our church planting team. Not everyone who met with us to pray helped us to start Koinonia House. Some felt called to remain at the church from which we were sent out but still came often to pray with us and offer support.

In July 2005, our family and a team of thirteen adults and several children were commissioned to begin Koinonia House. Brian Sauder attended the commissioning to accept us into the DOVE family and as a DOVE church.

Our journey as a church has been a rocky one . . . certainly not the smooth "dream" venture we had initially hoped for. We have never had our own building and have moved our meeting location seven times in nine years. It's become a bit of a joke among us. However, we've learned to be okay with the fact that things didn't go quite according to "our" plan.

In hindsight, we can see how much work God needed to do in us in this time, and we are quite sure He's still doing lots of teaching and renovation. We have had lots to learn, but one of the biggest lessons has been not to judge "success" by the world's standards, but rather, by weighing if we are being faithful to what God has called us to do. The things He calls us to—even things that fall under the umbrella of church planting—may look vastly different from the vision and plans He gives another church planter. We've had to learn to stop looking at others to gauge if we are doing well. Constantly we need to remember to look to Him alone for the "well done." Sometimes the things we want to do aren't actually the things He is asking us to do.

One of the hardest lessons has probably been to let go of our expectations and lay down our own desires (or what we think they should be), and seek out the desires of His heart. Often, we have found, the things we thought we wanted, we are thankful we didn't see come about . . . and we are incredibly blessed by embracing some things we thought that we would want nothing to do with. Along the course of our journey, for instance, there were two specific buildings we thought we should buy. At those times, we felt certain they would be perfect, only to discover in hindsight the properties either would quickly have been too small to accommodate our group or would have created major financial problems. We are thankful that God spared us from things we could not foresee.

There have also been dreams we were sure were God-given, and yet they seemed so impossible, we eventually just laid them down. When we started out, our "crazy" idea was to have church in a café as a "third place" where we could invite the community to come, hang out and find a safe and welcoming environment for both believers and non-believers. Years later, we are actually seeing some of this come about—not by our own doing but by God's orchestration in ways we could never have imagined. Although this dream did not happen in the way or timing that we had expected, we are in awe of God's better ways and better timing!

Even now, we are eagerly waiting to see what He will do next!

CHAPTER 10

This is our Story

Reaching our town in Pennsylvania, USA

Doug and Jen Lehman

Why Chambersburg? Why DOVE? Why us? Why are there so many broken people in our city who are not connected to Jesus or His church?

Not only do these questions demand answers but also demand prayer, passion and perseverance.

In November 2003, God unexpectedly dropped an idea in our hearts that He wanted us to plant a church in Chambersburg, Pennsylvania. Chambersburg is a great place to live with good people. It has a growing economy and plenty of healthy churches to attend . . . and yet that still small voice continued to whisper Chambersburg, unchurched, church plant to our hearts.

Throughout the winter and spring of 2004, we journeyed through the second semester of the DOVE Leadership and Ministry School. One Saturday in February we exited the building after listening to Merle Smucker from Gap, Pennsylvania share his church planting story. Jen and I sat in our Honda Accord in the Newport DOVE parking lot, looked at each other, and simultaneously said, "That is what we are called to do!" That day, the question changed from "why us," to "why not us?"

Needless to say, the call we received that day was just the beginning. It is a call that we continue to remember and lean on eleven years later, as we travel through the proverbial blood, sweat, tears and joys of church planting.

Several months after graduation, we began a mentoring relationship with Allen and Lucinda Dise. They prayed for us, encouraged us, challenged us and held us accountable to things that Holy Spirit had placed ,in our hearts. Allen and Lucinda helped us begin a relationship with the Newport DOVE congregation, which they pastored, and our family began to travel ninety minutes two times per month, so that we could be loved by the people of that congregation.

Eight years later, we stand in awe of what Jesus has done! We marvel at how He has taken a farmer and a homemaker from Chambersburg to begin a work that is impacting a city and beginning to impact nations.

During the summer of 2004, we began neighborhood picnics in our backyard with the intention of inviting our unchurched neighbors. During these evenings, we ate together, shared a devotional and prayed for each other. This was no small feat, since the majority of these people did not have a dynamic relationship with Jesus.

These biweekly gatherings consisted of 25 to 40 people and continued through early fall. When the weather turned colder, we moved these picnics to a local church building. Big mistake—only about one-third of the people traveled with us, and we lost most of our youth. Tragically, we began to call ourselves PLAYERS which stood for Purpose Loving Yeshua to Equip and Release Servants—probably a little too confusing of an attempt to be relevant to our culture.

Winter 2004/2005 was filled with new beginnings and painful loss when our friend and intercessor, Lucinda Dise, passed away. Jen and I purchased a new home consisting of three apartments, which we moved into in early February. God confirmed the transition to the new house one weekend in March, by sending someone to live next to us, who later joined the leadership of the church. That same weekend, Jen took the lady in the other apartment to a retreat where she met Jesus. The church plant was taking baby steps. The following Easter 2005, we began weekly meetings at Network Ministries, located in the heart of the community where we were called.

Beginning in June 2005, several young people, together with Jen and I began Tuesday night prayer gatherings on our front porch to intercede for our city. That summer became known as "The Summer on the Porch" and was the delivery room in which the church was birthed. These prayer and worship times quickly became the highlight of our week and would last two to four hours, sometimes followed by a walk to a local convenience store for a "shmuffin" after midnight. The Holy Spirit fell, and we met Jesus in powerful and tangible ways during those nights of prayer.

One night we were asking Jesus for a new name for our church. We wanted the name to clearly reflect our hearts. Our hearts desired that everything we did—work, worship and play—be a response to our relationship with Jesus. Someone mentioned the word overflow. Instantaneously, we knew the Holy Spirit had named us. We began calling ourselves Overflow Ministries, reflecting our desire that everything we say and do be an "overflow" of our relationship with Jesus.

God began to align hearts, and out of this group of young people came our first Leadership Team, as we began the tedious process of creating a wineskin to contain the vision and dreams that God had placed within our hearts. Newport DOVE commissioned us out as an official DOVE church plant in November of 2006.

Eight years later, we stand in awe of what Jesus has done! We marvel at how He has taken a farmer and a homemaker from Chambersburg, to begin a work that is impacting a city and beginning to impact nations.

CHAPTER 11

No casual Christian life for us

Planting churches in New England, USA

Gary and Bonnie Reiff

During my teenage years in the 1980s, my greatest fear was that I would lead just a "casual" Christian life. Although I desired to live 100 percent for Christ, I certainly did not start out with a vision to plant churches. Those seeds were planted when I accompanied a team to Peru, South America during the summer between my junior and senior years of college.

While working with South America Mission church planters in the jungle areas of Peru, a missionary couple shared their struggles in leaving all their friends and relatives behind and living in a remote village that required a 24-hour boat ride to reach them. These stories impacted me. While there, I read a book that inspired me to think about church planting.

Those seeds lay dormant until I was 29 years old. In the intervening years, I had attained my college degree, married Bonnie, began a career and we had our first child. My wife and I were elders at a church in West Haven, Connecticut. Revival was happening, people were coming to Christ, churches were growing. . . . During this time, my wife had a dream that we were to move to western Massachusetts to lead a church plant. It caught me by surprise, but we prayed about it, visited the area and God confirmed numerous times that this was His call for us.

Nonetheless, it was a big decision to quit my job and move more than an hour's drive from our friends.

Our former church had a really good worship team and great teaching from many well-known prophetic and inspirational speakers. We expected to pattern the church plant likewise and provide an atmosphere where the Holy Spirit could move freely. That first year, our church grew from about fifteen people to about thirty-five people, and then something happened. A church near us broke up and our gathering instantly doubled in size. Many of these new people were talented musicians. We gave them time to connect with us (three months) before they became part of our worship team. We also started having conferences with well-known speakers just like we had had at our former church. It seemed as if we were moving toward our destination; however, the way was not smooth and many changes needed to be made.

Build the church around the gifts and callings of the people who God has given you, rather than the needs of the church.

The first thing I learned was that people join a church for many reasons. We had come to identify ourselves as the prophetic, conference-style church in the region. When the nearby church fell apart, those members were also connected to the same prophetic, conference stream that we were a part of. I often visited their church, and I knew the leaders. They naturally gravitated to us when they needed another place to go. Our values of freedom, passionate worship, and the presence of the Holy Spirit were quickly embraced, but our church had become much more than that.

The small group of believers who made up our church met in small groups and connected relationally. I assumed new members would embrace these values, but many of them did not. Up to this point, I had never really connected my career in engineering to my work as pastor, but it hit me how the same things I enjoyed about engineering—designing and creating—were actually the same things I enjoyed about church ministry. I saw a need for common vision, common values and a church leadership that knew their calling and responsibilities.

This desire is what sparked an interest in DOVE and eventually led to our church formally becoming a partner church of DOVE. I found helpful resources in DOVE with their *Helping You Build Cell Churches*[1] book and the *Biblical Foundations Series.*[2] Our leadership team attended DOVE International Leadership Conferences held annually at Sandy Cove.

Those conferences and other DOVE events helped strengthen and encouraged our team, and we became part of the DOVE family of churches.

It's been eighteen years since we planted our first Massachusetts church. Since then, we have released that church to others to lead; we are currently planting house churches in New Hampshire.

From that first experience in church planting, the most important thing we learned is to keep it simple and focus on the things that matter most. In that first church plant, our leadership team ended up conducting three or more church meetings every week every week. We soon discovered that so many church meetings left us without much energy to reach out to neighbors and non-church friends. Today, we limit our church meetings to one per week. This enables members to become involved in non-church related activities where they can reach out and live their Christian life in the world.

Another essential truth we learned is to build the church around the gifts and callings of the people, rather than the needs of the church. In church ministry there is always a balance between the needs of the church and the gifts or interests of the people. I believe people burn out because they are doing something that they are not called to do and are put in roles that do not edify them. Although it's been said, "a good way to start someone out in ministry is to have them clean the bathrooms," I disagree. I understand the point that we often need to do jobs that we don't like and that helps us grow, but why not build the church around the gifts and callings of the people God has already given us. Keeping the church in the house and dividing up the house church ministry roles help balance the needs of the church. Our desire is to get everyone involved. Different people host, teach and share testimonies each week—which allows everyone to get involved.

In our church plants in Massachusetts and New Hampshire, we don't strive to be casual Christians but to live wholeheartedly every day of the week for God. That requires using our talents and gifts for God.

CHAPTER 12

Evangelistic zeal flourishes in Bulgaria

Tihomir and Dimka Tenev

I grew up in a Christian family when Bulgaria was ruled by Communism. In 1978 I married Dimka, and God blessed us with two wonderful children– Lydia and Danail.

During the Communist regime, my father became a pastor, but when the church started growing rapidly, the Communists forbade him to preach or pastor the church. As a family we were very active in the life of the church and in Bible smuggling, and because of that, we experienced different forms of persecution.

After the Iron Curtain fell at the end 1989, revival swept through Bulgaria from 1990 to the middle of 1992. In 1990, my wife and I had the privilege to study at a Bible college in England. In 1991, we returned to Bulgaria and formed an evangelistic team and quickly became immersed in spreading the gospel through mass evangelism. As a team, we held crusades at open air squares and stadiums with crowds between 20,000 to 40,000 people streaming forward to accept Jesus after each altar call. Miraculous healings were part of every crusade.

The religious freedom of Bulgaria allowed an influx of false religions and cults. The dangers of these cults were heavily covered by the media. Warnings were broadcast of the need to stay away from any religious activity, except by the established official Orthodox church in Bulgaria.

After forty-five years of Communism in Bulgaria, people had little knowledge of how to discern truth from false religions. Many became skeptical of every religion and no longer attended evangelistic events. It was clear that the time for mass evangelism in Bulgaria was over. In 1993, God spoke to our hearts and we planted a church in Sliven (the city in which we live) with the purpose of making disciples of Jesus. During the mass evangelism we had preached to thousands of people, and now we had only twenty to thirty people. It was difficult now to preach to empty chairs in the hall!

In 1995, God gave us the strategy of the cell church structure. After two years of preparation, we were able to make the transition to a cell church. In 1998, we were invited to attend a cell church conference in America where we met Larry Kreider. The following year, Larry visited our church in Bulgaria. I was touched by his father's heart and his willingness to help us achieve the vision God has given us as a church. In 1999, we became a part of the DOVE family of churches, and, because of this wonderful relationship, we decided to change the name of our church to DOVE Christian Fellowship Bulgaria.

Today the church in Sliven has fifteen small groups. Thirty-two leaders of these small groups help pastor the church. Working through small groups is completely different than having a program-based large church. People are much more receptive to visiting a small group where they know each other, than attending a mass meeting where just a few people know them. We believe God has given us this biblical structure, and the only thing we are sorry about is that we did not know about it earlier.

We are so happy for the life the church has on a weekly basis. On Sunday, a main celebration is conducted. During the week, every small group has its own gathering for fellowship and for serving each other, by practicing what they have learned from the Bible. But the real life of building the church happens in between these two meetings. People meet individually or as couples and learn how to develop a personal relationship with God, live for Him and make disciples.

Serving God in Bulgaria no longer requires risking one's physical life, but our zeal for the Lord has not diminished.

We have planted two more churches in other cities of Bulgaria. One of those churches planted three more small groups in different cities in Bulgaria, with the purpose of becoming churches.

In 2005 my wife and I transferred the leadership of the church in Sliven to our son Danail, who serves as senior pastor with his wife, Nora. Since then, my wife and I are committed to spiritual overseeing and spiritual parenting. At the moment, we are overseeing five congregations in Bulgaria, plus the one in Sliven, which is the mother church of DOVE Bulgaria.

Serving God in Bulgaria no longer requires risking one's physical life, but our zeal for the Lord has not diminished. I do not know if there will be another revival, but I am believing with all of my heart that with or without revival, with or without any freedom—we, as a church of the living God, and as His disciples and followers, will always do what Jesus instructs us in Mathew 28:19-20. "Therefore go and make disciples of all nations, baptizing them in the name of the Father and of the Son and of the Holy Spirit, and teaching them to obey everything I have commanded you. And surely I am with you always, to the very end of the age."

CHAPTER 13

God rocks our world in Ireland

No one grows more through a church plant than the planters themselves

Rachel and James Krechnyak Jr.

Our call to church planting came over stir-fry food and lattes. During a casual dinner discussion, a church leader reached across the table and said, "God already said to go. We should not ask 'if' but 'when' and 'how.'"

Within a few months, Rachel and I started a monthly prayer meeting in Portlaoise, a town of 20,000 in Ireland, which had no Spirit-filled church. We were no strangers to this town, thirty minutes drive from where we lived; we had prayed there randomly on numerous occasions. Through a series of phone calls, three local people showed up to our first meeting. As the months passed, we added Bible studies, five mission values and a church name. On October 10, 2004, we officially launched with twelve committed people.

We gathered mostly with those who had little experience in our "type" of church. What was lacking in qualifications and training was surpassed in enthusiasm. But as a young family, we were often engulfed with a contradiction between anticipation for good things coming, coupled with a sense of isolation and weariness.

Our first year, I had some serious health issues. The pressures had unlocked hidden fears deep within my soul, and what oozed from those emotional sores took its toll on me physically. Through faith and prayer, I was healed over a six-year period of struggles.

I determined to live what we were trying to impart into other people's lives through discipleship. I wanted to be transparent and create an environment, saturated in grace, in which each person could say of themselves that they could do what we do. Multiplication had to start at a grassroots level. As we sought to be intentional about training, empowering and releasing, we have been forced to press beyond our resources and comfort. In our fourth year, we renovated a two-story warehouse, three years later planted a second church and more recently have gone to two services. We are anticipating planting at least three more churches during the next few years. Our next major hurdle is transitioning from having planted two churches to becoming a church planting movement.

It is amazing how often we look to dramatic experiences, grandiose vision or major steps as decisive moments in our lives, but more often than not, it is in the context of ordinary faithfulness that God's

Word reaches into the depth of our soul and rocks our world. In retrospect, it is plain to see how during an ordinary dinner discussion, God used the church leader's admonition to "go" and not ask "if" but "when." We can even see how God orchestrated our childhoods as preparation for our ministry.

When I was about five years old, my parents stepped out of lapsed Catholicism into a burning passion for Jesus during the Charismatic Movement. I do not remember when I became a Christian. I find it hard to remember when Jesus was not part of my life. My childhood relationship with God was labeled by classmates in the sarcastically affectionate nickname "Pope James." In some curious fashion, my nickname foreshadowed the path my life would take. Little did I know that in Ireland, my future bride was having her own personal experiences with God, lining her teddies in rows and delivering fiery sermons to them.

It is amazing how often we look to dramatic experiences, grandiose vision or major steps as decisive moments in our lives, but more often than not, it is in the context of ordinary faithfulness that God's Word reaches into the depth of our soul and rocks our world.

At age fifteen, I watched with bated breath and intrigue as the first sledgehammer blow struck the Berlin Wall. Five years later, I took my first mission trip to war–torn Croatia, resulting in changing my course of study in Bible College. Outreaches followed: In 1994, Romania; 1995, Jamaica; 1996, Hungary, Serbia, and Croatia.

In 1999, with my bride to be, whom I met in Youth With A Mission, we poised ourselves to move to her homeland. A generation after my mother immigrated to America as a refugee from Hungary post World War II, I was immigrating from America to Europe, simply determined by simplistic obedience to, "Give it a few years and see what happens." Four years later, we had that life-altering dinner conversation.

We have learned that no one grows more through a church plant than the planters themselves. In hindsight, the deepest lessons have been those of greater dependency on God. We want to live in love with one another, and yet we do not want our discipleship community to become our primary focus, rather than reaching out to the unchurched. Our failures and mistakes, those things we would love to avoid, have been keys to greater humility and the development of interdependency within our community. For that reason, we would change nothing. If anything, we are compelled to trust God in greater measure, and to relax more with who we are and the process of getting to where we are going. In our weakness, His strength is manifest!

CHAPTER 14

The crossroads that would not go away

Church Planting in Virginia, USA

Bobby and Wanda Alger

Church plants begin by either default or by design. Ours was a little of both. Wanda and I had grown up in the same denomination. Before we met and married, she had helped plant a church that grew to 1,500 in attendance and spread into four locations within the county where we resided in Virginia. After Wanda and I had married, we sensed God calling us out of that church.

Now, the default: Having settled the fact that God was calling us out, the next question was "to where"? On the Sunday we resigned, a seasoned intercessor approached us and said that the word "crossroads," applied to us. For the next few months, we sought the Lord as to where this might be by visiting towns and cities, but with no confirmation. One Sunday afternoon, Wanda's father called us. He said that he had just read Jeremiah 6:16 and thought it might be for us. This verse states, "Stand at the crossroads, ask for the godly ways, walk in it, and you will find rest for your souls." I remembered that a year earlier because we had received a Christmas picture from a congregational member with that verse on it!

Maybe the default was being designed by the Holy Spirit? We decided to revisit a nearby town (one hour away) for the second time. This time we stopped by the Chamber of Commerce. In reading the history of the town, half way down the page the paragraph started with the words: "Winchester is known today as a strategic crossroads area of the civil war and commerce." We immediately sensed the affirmation of the Holy Spirit and, soon after, relocated with our family to Winchester where we purchased property and planted Crossroads Community Church.

As confirmation of His word, God provided our financial needs without having to seek additional work. Our housing came through several friends, financial blessings came from a church planting grant, and generous monthly donations from former congregational members came in without my wife and I ever asking for any! For a number of years, a businessman tithed one of his multiple businesses to our church plant, so we started out being fully supported! In addition to our family of five, two single adults moved with us, and a family from a neighboring town joined the church planting venture.

It was a home church in every sense of the word! Church was in our home, my office was in the home and my wife home-schooled our children. For the first six months it was stir-crazy in the home. Despite that,

God was drawing people and lives were being changed. After becoming friends with a local pastor, we moved our small fellowship to his church building on Sunday nights, then to Saturday nights for a larger space. After one year from launch, we began Sunday morning services and doubled our attendance. Finally, after seven different locations in seven years, we transformed a warehouse space in a local plaza, which now anchors Crossroads Community Church.

Crossroads Community Church may have been planted by both default and by design, but its focus remains the same: "Stand at the crossroads, ask for the godly ways, walk in it, and you will find rest for your souls."

These are some of the lessons we learned along the way:

- Those you think will help you plant, won't.

- Those you don't expect to help, will.

- You won't attract who you want, but you will attract who you are.

- It's not what you start that's important, it is what you can sustain that makes the difference.

- Having a written plan is a must. God can always change it, but if it's not written down, it has no credibility to others.

- Small groups are vital for a quality start. They become more difficult to maintain as Sunday morning services require lots of energy to manage.

- Once something is working—don't change it until you have a clear track to switch to.

These are some of the mistakes we made along the way:

- We stopped a monthly leadership gathering because a few people thought it was unproductive. Due to this, we lost traction and communication with those who truly valued it.

- We did not give as much attention to the small groups as we did to the large group. Though our culture looks at the large meeting as priority, it is in the small groups where people truly feel at home.

- Discipleship got crowded out by the busyness of people's schedules. Many who start well, don't finish well, because they do not have the tools for the long haul.

Some things we did right:

- We stayed relational in all things! Even if vision and methodologies differ, friendships can endure changes and differences.

- We offered appointments to help people find personal freedom from past hurts. This is a critical ministry to a healthy church family.

- We focused on maintaining a healthy leadership core. We gave leaders opportunities to grow in areas of their interests and to train and equip them to follow their call. Healthy leaders produce healthy churches.

- We connected with other like-minded churches and community organizations. To be a king-dom-minded ministry means to see the church beyond our own congregation.

Finally, after two years, we became a partner with DOVE. When we first planted Crossroads, we were aligned with the denomination and the church movement with which we had been involved former-ly. We soon realized that our dual connection with the denomination and movement wasn't working. We needed mentorship in a new direction. Before we planted Crossroads, Wanda and I had attended several cell-based conferences where Larry Kreider was a featured speaker. We connected with his heart and view of ministry. So, when our advisory team decided it was time to realign, our first choice was DOVE. Wanda and I met with Ron Myer and our hearts attached. We found friends, family and home.

Crossroads Community Church may have been planted by both default and by design, but its focus remains the same: "Stand at the crossroads, ask for the godly ways, walk in it, and you will find rest for your souls."

CHAPTER 15

Stretching boundaries in Mysore, India

Multi-cultural church represents 17 nations

Philip and Kerina Omondi

We are amazed at what the Lord is doing in Mysore, India. People representing seventeen nations and many different religions attend Destiny Centre Mysore. The Lord is stretching our boundaries and giving us faith to reach the nations of the world.

Destiny Centre Mysore started in 2000 when some like-minded university students and I sensed God calling us to start a multi-cultural church. We were on fire for Jesus, but we had no mentorship or spiritual covering.

I was a young, unmarried student at the time, and the bulk of responsibilities fell on me. I tried to do what I sensed God wanted, but I often felt so stressed from carrying the body alone, plus all my studies and carrying on a courtship with my soon-to-be wife, Kerina.

When a friend introduced me to Hesbone Odindo, who leads a DOVE Church, I sensed such a kinship with him. We shared common values for building relationships and reaching people groups.

Hesbone introduced me to Ibrahim Omondi, DOVE Africa apostolic leader. Hesbone and Ibrahim prayed for me and helped me with some needs. I felt so connected with them, and I realized I needed a family, a spiritual covering.

However, since Kerina and I planned to marry, we needed to return to our homeland in Kenya to renew our visas. The immigration law required us to remain in Africa for two years before we were able to return to India. Kerina and I married in 2005, and returned to India in 2007.

We must not limit God to the present little thing we are doing, because the Lord is stretching our boundaries and has given us faith to reach the world. We are amazed at what God is doing.

By that time, attendance at Destiny had dropped. We entered into a one-year engagement period with DOVE. DOVE's focus on cell churches made it easy for people to connect and our numbers started growing. At a DOVE Africa Conference, I had met Greg Linnebach, a DOVE Mission International (DMI) associate from Arizona. He served as a mentor, and I appreciated that Ibrahim Omondi and Larry Kreider came to help us.

Our church is made up of mostly college students, who will return to their own countries after their studies and are eager to plant churches there. We already are planning church plants in India, Namibia and Zambia. We also have an outreach to the Siddi people groups in remote villages. The cell church concept enables small groups to grow and multiply more rapidly than establishing an actual church building. Also believers are more accepting in becoming house church leaders rather than assuming leadership of a church. We don't see cells as another program in the church—we see cells as the actual church.

We have five cell churches that meet during the week. On Sunday, we meet as one large group. These meetings are attended by students and families representing seventeen nations such as Nepal, Syria, Iran, Sri Lanka, India and several African countries.

We lift up Jesus and give a clear biblical message, which one might think would be repulsive to the Muslim, Hindu and Buddhist followers. Instead, several of them have expressed similar statements as one Muslim who said, "I attend because I feel something different in this church than anywhere else. There is some kind of power here." Many attending say they are inspired by the worship and sharing.

Students invite their friends. Sports evangelism is a big part of church growth. Some attendees face persecution after becoming Christians. Some believers are not allowed to attend formal church but can attend informal gatherings such as cell churches.

To remain in India with student visas, my wife and I must continue our studies at the university. Both of us have several degrees. I love my wife and our two children, Rebekah Krupa, 8, and our son, Abhishek Israel, almost 3. My wife and I are committed to each other and to spending quality time with our children. Teaching this by example is a novel concept among many cultures, but one that we really promote.

We must not limit God to the present little thing we are doing because the Lord is stretching our boundaries and has given us faith to reach the world. We are amazed at what God is doing.

CHAPTER 16

No plans to start a house church

Hungry for more in Pennsylvania, USA

Brian and Kim Zimmerman

We didn't plan on starting a house church. To be honest, it started us.

We were fine just showing up each week, doing our part in leadership of a local church. And then we weren't fine. Something in us began to burn with a deeper hunger for more, for intentional relationship. We found ourselves with the younger generation coming and asking us to show them how to find a deeper walk with God and His Word. We began to ask God, "Is there more than this? Is there more to just being somewhere each Sunday?"

In the midst of these questions, we began to ask others whether it was possible to have a setting where people came together, shared life, shared the Word and could pursue God, but without the typical format of a Sunday morning service. Not that there is anything wrong with that structure, but we wanted more—more family, more Word, more ability to ask and learn.

We started meeting weekly with three to four friends—reading through books of the Bible, talking, praying and changing. More people started attending and coming earlier and earlier each week, so we began to share our meal with them. In turn, they started bringing food to share, so we ended up having weekly meals with this growing family, and then reading and living the Word together.

This ragamuffin group that began innocently and organically started to become something we couldn't define. We just knew it was new. We

We wanted more— more family, more Word, more ability to ask and learn.

had heard of house churches, even read Larry Kreider's book *House to House*[1] and probably twenty other books on house church, but we didn't plan on starting a house church or beginning a house church network. We didn't consider ourselves church planters. We were just hungry for more of what God had for us, and we began to do what He was giving us naturally and organically. It wasn't until we ran into Larry and LaVerne at a conference in Lancaster and shared what was on our heart and what was happening in our home, that Larry gently told us, "You have a house church."

One of the principles we have learned is that a house church is always fluid and needs to be willing to move in whatever direction the Holy Spirit tells us. The common mistake is to take a traditional Sunday morning church service and try to fit it into a house church. We have found that each week is different in respect to what is happening in each other's lives, what we are studying and what is happening in our culture. When someone is hurting, we can take our whole gathering to minister to them. When we all gather together and sense that we need a night of prayer, we can do that.

Mistakes—we've made a few. But I think that if we stay teachable and humble, any mistake can produce a positive result. We have come to understand that we are disciples making disciples. We have Bible studies that meet outside of our weekly gathering; these include some people who are not part of our house church. We also have joined our youth with other youth in The New Initiative, the house church network we are a part of, to create a "fusion" of youth. This is a youth group for all of the youth who are part of the house churches in The New Initiative.

We are beginning a new direction to help our group multiply. We meet three weeks at our home (the host home for Shift Church) then on the fourth week, we break into four to six groups that meet in each other's homes, some meeting on different days. This helps not only with multiplication, but also increases the possibility of reaching more people. For example, we meet on a Wednesday night, but on that fourth week several groups chose to meet on a Sunday morning. This enables them to invite others who do not attend a church and encourages growth in each group, with the intent to become house churches branching off of Shift.

What would we do differently? Not much except we desire to keep the size smaller for each house church. We currently have between 35 to 45 people attending, which is a large number to gather together for a meal and fellowship. The heart of a house church is relational and that seems to work best with twenty or less. That is why multiplication is key to a house church, to keep the flow and keep the growth healthy.

We value and do outward missions in the following ways. We participate in "Love Lititz," where we adopt a home and help with whatever the needs of that homeowner are, such as painting, mulching and picking up groceries. We also serve a lunch monthly in Lancaster city to the hurting and the homeless. We realize that each of us is doing missions where we live, work and play—but there are benefits of working together as a body.

We didn't plan on starting a house church. It has indeed, started us.

CHAPTER 17

Growing is in the going

THE GATHERING in Ontario, Canada

Philip and Lisa Wright

There is a beautiful verse of scripture in the book of Malachi that goes like this: "But unto you that fear my name shall the Sun of righteousness arise with healing in his wings; and you shall go forth, and grow up as calves of the stall" (Mal. 4:2 KJV). Take a look at the last part of that verse, "and you shall go forth, and grow up."

Our idea is that we grow up first, obtain knowledge, get comfortable in our skin and "really feel ready", and then off we go. That sounds like conventional wisdom, but that's not necessarily God's idea. He said, go forth first, and then you will grow up. God's motto is "Growing is in the going!" And going isn't necessarily heading off to some geographical destination; in most cases, it simply means to get started doing what you feel God has placed in your heart to do. That's basically the story of The Gathering and perhaps, it's your story too.

When my wife, Lisa, and I started our house church in 2002, my heart was in the right place, but God had to do some major work on my head. Prior to this time I had been the senior pastor of two churches, from 1984 to 1996, in what we consider typical or traditional church structure. Then I travelled fulltime in ministry from 1997-2001, speaking and teaching in churches and conferences. Beginning in 2002, Lisa and I started a church plant in Woodstock, Ontario, which developed into a deliberate focus of the house church model.

When in casual conversations with the pastors in our town or with other Christians, the question would inevitably arise: "Where is your church located"? Suddenly I would find myself hyperventilating and my words would get caught in my throat, "Ahh . . . it's in my house." I felt embarrassed to admit that. A pastor in our town told some folks in his church that what we were doing wasn't a real church; it was "just a Bible Study." This guy didn't think

"Where is your church located"? Suddenly I would find myself hyperventilating and my words would get caught in my throat, "Ahh . . . it's in my house." I felt embarrassed to admit that.

that we were a church, but really, how could I fault him—I wasn't even sure myself. How could I convince others that what we were doing was okay when I wasn't even convinced myself!

Thankfully, today I feel secure in the fact that what we are doing is what God wants. I love the simplicity and the ease in which we are able to communicate with one another.

I learned many wonderful things on this journey. But one important principle was realizing that those

whom God had sent to us did not see everything the
same way I did.

I was convinced that in a brief span of time
the others in our small group would begin house
churches themselves, and I taught with that expecta-
tion in mind. Don't get me wrong, church planting is
certainly a great thing: it is biblical and needed. But
Lisa gave me a more balanced view when she pointed
out that God created us with a variety of goals, gifts
and drives, and that I needed to stop my relentless
push to cause this to happen.

Paul makes this variety of gifts abundantly clear in
Romans 12:4, 6-8: "For as we have many members in
one body, and all members have not the same office.
. . . Having then gifts differing according to the grace
that is given to us, whether prophecy, let us prophesy
according to the proportion of faith; or ministry, let us
wait on our ministering: or he that teaches, on teaching;
or he that exhorts, on exhortation: he that gives, let him
do it with simplicity; he that rules, with diligence; he
that shows mercy, with cheerfulness."

After I pulled that beam out of my eye, I was
amazed by what I saw and wondered how I had
missed it. I rejoice and love to listen to how these
blessed people have an impact in our community and
beyond—whether it be through interactions with
those they work with or among family members or
friends; divine appointments that happen in the most
curious of ways; through loving and mentoring "at
risk youth" and on and on and on. . . .

CHAPTER 18

Stop focusing on numbers

Divine connections build church in Missouri, USA

Sharon and Jim Allen

Seven years ago, my husband Jim and I started a house church with ten people. Today we have three healthy house churches. One multiplied from our house church, and we planted a house church in Hays, Kansas. Two of these house churches are ready to multiply again.

When our first house church began, the attendance really fluctuated. One Sunday we would have ten, the next week maybe four to six—and fear would set in. My husband and I would question, "Did we really hear God call us to do this?" So back to the prayer closet we would go.

The Lord told us to stop focusing on numbers and become involved in the lives of the people who were attending and see them healed and set free to help others. When we started interceding before the Lord and doing spiritual warfare against the enemy, people's hearts were healed and set free. When someone feels the love of Jesus, gets set free and emotionally healed, they tell people, and that draws more people.

My husband and I have been a part of the DOVE family for almost twenty years. In 1995, Jim and I planted one of the first cell-based DOVE churches in the USA outside of Pennsylvania. We started with about twenty-five people. Those were exciting years. Looking back, we probably had more zeal than wisdom. Jim has a pastoral gift. Wherever he is, the love of Jesus is there. But after ten years, Jim felt burned out. He didn't see people getting set free, and that burdened him. We attended another church for more than a year, but kept our relationship with the DOVE family. Larry Kreider encouraged us to start a house church, this time in Kansas City, where we had moved. Larry also gave us a copy of his book *Starting a House Church.*[1]

At first, I resisted. All I saw was too much work. We have two biological children, three adopted children and twelve grandchildren. I also struggled with the need to give up some things—such as our plan for retirement and traveling. But I recognized that anything in life worth having requires sacrifice. I sensed the Lord's calling and also the faith that He would be there to build if we would follow Him. It sounded so easy; yet, a deeper revelation is that we only surrender to the degree we obey!

Jim also believed that when we started a house church, the Lord wanted us to change roles—I should become the senior elder and Jim would assist me. I wasn't so sure he had heard that right. Some people resist the idea of women being senior elders. At the same time, Jim and I realized the importance of operating in our gifts and as a team. Leaders confirmed that I have an apostolic and teaching gift. Sometimes I found myself speaking so bluntly. I really need to let the Lord prune me to speak in love and concern for others, so as not to hurt them. We also realized some of Jim's previous burnout was the result of feeling stressed from senior elder duties.

Walking in our gifting has helped our marriage, family and church. On Sunday mornings, Jim and I are a team. Jim is at the door greeting people, laughing and bringing the love of Jesus into the room, making sure all the people's immediate needs are met. I am listening to the needs of the people and discerning how to train them to function in the Kingdom of God versus the kingdom of the world.

Stop focusing on numbers and become involved in the lives of people to see them healed and set free to help others. . . that draws people.

We are a church without walls and meet in houses—not a church building. When Jim and I caught a vision for establishing a church without walls, it completely changed our focus. Our house churches have become intensive care units to heal and free people.

We have learned, house church isn't for everyone. I believe when leaders have a pure heart and clean hands and are confident in whom they belong to, God will create divine connections to build the church. People who have the power and authority of Christ in their lives are excited about sharing Jesus and their excitement is contagious.

CHAPTER 19

And the church grew

*Expanding in Lebanon, Schuylkill and Berks
counties, Pennsylvania, USA*

Ron and Bonnie Myer

Bonnie and I attended a DOVE church for the
first time in August 1982. From the moment we
walked through the doors and experienced the worship and ministry of the Word, we were convinced
that the Lord was calling us to be a part of what He
was doing in the DOVE family.

We joined a local cell group, which just happened to meet two miles from our house. We began
to experience spiritual mothering and fathering for
the first time in our lives. Our cell group leaders
were so patient with us and taught us so much about
the Kingdom while discipling us and teaching us
to make disciples. Soon we were asked to become
assistant cell leaders and then lead the cell group. Although we felt unqualified, it was an exciting time as
we trusted in the Lord for His guidance and leadership. By the grace of God, the cell thrived and multiplied with three cells planted in Lebanon County and
two in Berks County by 1986.

In the summer of 1986, we were asked to be part of a team to plant a church on the border of Lebanon and Berks counties with the purpose of growing and releasing future church plants. While we certainly didn't feel qualified, we accepted and helped plant the new celebration. We assumed primary leadership of what was then called Northern Celebration and later renamed Lebanon-Berks Celebration. The church grew. People were saved and discipled. They reached out to others, and the Kingdom was growing.

During those years, Bonnie and I owned a 225-cow dairy farm with 300 acres of land. We were able to be part of the exciting church planting venture because we had wonderful people serving alongside us. But with ministry demands expanding, I was encouraged by both family and spiritual leaders around me to hear from the Holy Spirit as to whether Bonnie and I should sell the farm to be able to focus our energies on church ministry. This was one of the hardest decisions I have ever had to make, as the farm was the fulfillment of a life dream which I had since I was a child. However, it became clear that it was time to give up my life's dream to fulfill my life's call. We sold the cattle in the fall of 1987 and the equipment and land the following year.

And the church grew! People were being added weekly and impacting the community. In 1990, the church sent a number of families to become part of a DOVE plant in Schuylkill County. By 1994, the Lebanon-Berks church had grown to 400 people. We met in an old elementary school. Every Sunday for seven years, we had to set up chairs, sound system, platform, and then clear everything out after the service. The condition of the building and the inconvenience it caused demonstrates more fully that where the Spirit of the Lord is, people will come.

In 1995, the church was ecstatic that the Lord had blessed us to the place where we could commission a group of people to plant a church in Berks County. Although it was exciting to be the sending church, I was unprepared for the disappointment of the people who were left behind. We had commissioned out some of our best people, and we missed them.

But the church grew! Through the course of events, we moved to another location as an interim until we located a building in the center of Lebanon city, which is where we wanted to be. A number of years later, we moved to another location in the city. And the church grew!

During that time, Bonnie and I again felt the Lord's prompting that a change was coming. For a number of years I had been hearing prophetic words of "you are a pastor to pastors" and "the Lord is calling you to be a leader to leaders" and similar confirmations. In January of 1999, Bonnie and I felt directed of the Lord to transition out of being the pastor of a local church and devote all of our energies into apostolic ministry. We turned leadership over to a capable couple in August 1999. By June 2001 another couple sensed God's calling to plant a church in Myerstown. About sixty-five people were sent out from DOVE Lebanon to Myerstown. People were saved, discipled and added to the church. After a number of years of fruitful ministry in Myerstown, the church grew to about 200 people with sixteen small groups. Again, there was a stirring to plant another church.

In 2009, a new church was planted in the same town where the original church had been planted in 1987. Talk about the Lord coming full circle! When we originally responded to the call to be part of a church plant in 1986, we had no idea that God's graciousness would enable us to see additional churches planted in Schuylkill, Berks and Lebanon counties.

Bonnie and I rejoice in the passion and desire shown by new church planters all over the world. Who knows who, where and how the Lord will continue to expand His Kingdom?

CHAPTER 20

Adopted by the DOVE family

No longer an island in Duncannon, Pennsylvania, USA

Matthew and Bethany Zang

Although we were not a DOVE church plant, we are now part of the DOVE family through adoption. In June 1999, some faithful believers and I planted a new work in Duncannon, Pennsylvania. We stepped out in faith and obedience to follow God's purpose, and He brought us a long way. However, we faced many challenges because we had no denomination or church planting agency to assist us.

All we had was faith and the call of God. With His help we were able to accomplish His purpose in a church plant, but I knew I needed counsel and wisdom from others to mature my calling and ministry. I longed for it but did not know where to look or what to do.

About four years ago while reading the book, *The Biblical Role of Elders for Today's Church*,[1] I sensed the still small voice of the Spirit say to me, "you need to partner with DOVE International." Not knowing anything about DOVE International, I did not pursue it. However, in November of 2013, I was reading another book published through DOVE: *Five-Fold*

Ministry Made Practical.[2] Again, I heard the still small voice of the Spirit of God, "Align yourself with DOVE International."

This time I did not ignore it. I went privately to my pastoral staff and explained that I believed that God was positioning us, as a church, to come under a spiritual umbrella. Without my mentioning DOVE, our Administrative Pastor said, "I believe we should come under DOVE International." The next day we searched for information on DOVE International and contacted Ron Myer. With the leading of the Holy Spirit, we as a team of elders were able to impart this understanding into the congregation and receive general consensus. We have been engaged for almost a year, and we are really enjoying being part of a family. We learned that we need a spiritual umbrella—a mother and father.

Abundant Harvest Church is no longer an island but a part of a family of churches that strengthen and encourage one another. We are a healthy and vibrant congregation of believers worshiping and serving His purposes in the earth.

CHAPTER 21

Leverage opportunities

Micro-church planted in Oregon, USA

Tim and Angie Wenger

Angie and I were both raised in Christian homes. Our dads were pastors, and we decided to follow Jesus at a young age. We attended Elim Bible Institute in New York for a year and married at the young age of 19 and 20. Rather than return to Bible school, we were led by God to move to McMinnville, Oregon and invest our time and energy into a local church.

In our early twenties, we began to sense the first shades of a desire for church planting. Our church was transitioning into a cell church, and we were finding great fulfillment and success in developing the youth ministry totally around cell groups. Yet I realized that there were many leaders that had a pastoral calling that were called to lead a larger number of people than a cell group and find fulfillment of their calling by being the elder in an actual church. Hebrews 13:17 became very meaningful to me as I pondered how to develop a church structure that would release as many elders (pastor-shepherds) as possible, who had the authority, passion and character to "watch over peoples' souls" and give an account for those souls before the Chief Shepherd. At the time, I was drawn to house church networks.

After twenty years of building houses, directing a discipleship school and raising a family, we begin to sense God leading us towards planting a church. We were blessed to be a part of a community of persons with the same passion. In 2010, the board members of The Mandate Discipleship School sensed God leading us to venture out in faith into this new endeavor. We decided to sell our homes and relocate to a new town where we could work together in church planting. The Holy Spirit led other families and individuals to join us, moving from various towns in Oregon.

I personally struggled with doubt and fear. Are we hearing God correctly? What if folks sold their homes and moved, and it didn't work out? Angie, along with other leaders in my life, were a constant source of support and encouragement and regularly affirmed that we were to move forward. We realized God's call on our life and were compelled to follow His lead despite the risk.

We planted The Hive micro-church network in Corvallis, Oregon and joined DOVE International for our oversight. We feel God led us to DOVE because of their focus on being a church planting movement with some of the same values as The Hive such as Anabaptist roots, the Holy Spirit empowering, apostolic oversight, building and planting "underground churches" and reaching the nations.

Corvallis is a college town with a population of more than 50,000, and has a large foreign student population, many from countries that are closed to the gospel of Jesus Christ.

Some of the reasons we chose the micro church network model, where churches of 30 to 70 persons network together, is because it enables the following:

- leadership development with the planting of new churches

- structure is lightweight and easier to reproduce and lead

- churches can meet in large homes or rented facilities

- group is large enough that each age has someone to relate to but not small enough to result in homogenization

- size enables greater participation for people to offer a Psalm, prophecy, teaching, etc.

- Elders can lead the church and still work fultime, thus not needing paid staff.

Some things that God has been teaching us include the following:

- Set up oversight: We did not want to build our church with folks who were ungovernable and anti-authority. As leaders, we sought to deal with that attitude in our own lives. Choosing to have functioning oversight embedded that principle into our community and is bearing good fruit.

- We wanted to reduce activities that did little to contribute towards evangelism and discipleship. People are overwhelmed with life and busyness, so we eliminated all but the most essential. We guard against too many inward-focused meetings that crowd out connecting with non-believers and one-on-one discipling and mentoring.

- We promote gatherings of twos and threes for accountability, discipleship and mentoring.

- We welcome people to live with us and observe our lives. This principle seems to be one of the most effective strategies for evangelism and discipleship in our day. "God sets the solitary in families" (Psalm 68:6).

- If a church planter is not apostolic, they need to get under the regular influence of this gifting.

- Use a wide range of persons to teach the Scriptures on a regular basis. We don't want everyone going off on their own little "personal talking tangent." Therefore, all of our micro-churches teach on the same book of the Bible.

- Actively promote worship that is participatory, celebratory, focused on Jesus and not introspective.

Alas, we are not yet seeing people making first-time decisions for Jesus to the degree that we had hoped. This is probably our biggest weakness. We pray for it, we equip for it and trust that the Lord will honor our efforts.

A large part of our focus is to send folks to un-reached places in the world that have never heard of Jesus. In Corvallis, we put a lot of effort into our discipleship school. The Mandate Discipleship School[1] has become an engine of growth and has assisted in drawing a number of singles in their early twenties to Corvallis to be a part of a spiritual family. Those who are not in the discipleship school live in community and become involved in accountability groups and in mentoring relationships. God has blessed us with a lot of healthy marriages and families and we want to leverage this opportunity by welcoming those who do not have a family into our families and church community.

CHAPTER 22

USA house church grows into international movement

Starting a new church was not even on my radar.

Larry and LaVerne Kreider

You have just read many examples and stories of church planting around the world. Let me share the story of the very first DOVE church plant, which became the seed for many of those you have just read about.

As I write this manuscript, my mind races back to forty years ago when I was in my mid-twenties. At that time, starting a new church was not even on my radar. A group of us had reached out to some unchurched teens in our area. Many of these teens gave their lives to Christ, and we were committed to helping them grow in the Lord. LaVerne and I were firmly established in a local church in our community.

Had you told me then that we would eventually build a team and start a new church, I would have told you that was a crazy idea. After all, I had no seminary experience or even a desire to start a new church. In the 1970s, a group of us from our church youth group had a burden to reach out in love to the unchurched youth of our local community in northern Lancaster County, Pennsylvania. During this time, youth throughout the United States were turning to God in record numbers after a decade of tumult in which many had sought answers for life by dabbling in the occult and drugs. We set out to initiate creative and culturally effective ways to reach young people with the love of Jesus. Through friendship evangelism, dozens of young people began coming to Jesus.

A weekly Bible study was established for these new believers, and I was asked to lead this group. We taught simple truths from scripture and encouraged believers to love Jesus with all of their hearts. In this informal group setting, many began to experience a genuine relationship with Jesus and a growing depth of relationship with each other.

Although the team working with us did their best to help the new believers find church homes, most of them simply did not fit into the established churches. During this time, God spoke to me in prayer and asked if I was willing to be involved in the "underground church." I interpreted underground church to mean small groups of believers meeting in homes (underground, in a manner of speaking) to pray, evangelize and build relationships with each other. These small groups would provide the opportunity for people to experience a Christian faith built on relationships, not on structured meetings. In these informal settings, people could share their lives with each other and reach out with the healing love of Jesus to a broken world. We desired to follow the pattern in the New Testament church as modeled in the book of Acts, where the believers met from house to house.

We studied the Scriptures to discover the necessary components of a church from God's perspective. We knew that if two or three gather in His name, He is in the midst of us. But we also realized that the church is certainly more than two or three meeting for a Bible study. We needed more answers, which we found in Acts 2:38-47.

According to these scriptures, a local church in the book of Acts was made up of those who had repented of their sins and received Jesus Christ as Lord. They were connected to leadership in the whole body of Christ (they taught the Apostles' doctrine). They did not need a building because they often met in homes (house to house). They prayed together and experienced the power of God in their midst, they shared life together and they served one another. Church was a spiritual family, and families need parents, so the leaders took on the role of being a spiritual parent! People came to Christ every day and joined these new spiritual families. We wanted to experience church like they did in the book of Acts!

We started the first home group, and soon our house was packed with young people. We trained leaders to take over the initial home group, and we started a second group in our brother-in-law's and sister's home. A few young couples committed to discipling new believers led each group.

At this point, we did not consider our two Bible study groups to be a church. However, during a Sunday morning service at our local church, I sensed the Lord calling me to start a new kind of church for new believers. New churches must be birthed in prayer, so I invited twelve to fifteen believers, mostly from the two home groups, along with a few others who had a heart for church planting to meet at 5:00 a.m. every Saturday morning to pray. We prayed for wisdom to start a new church—a new wineskin (Luke 5:38)— one that is appropriate to serve and disciple these new believers in Jesus.

After months of prayer and receiving counsel from our local church leaders, the Lord released us to begin. In October 1980, about twenty-five of us gathered in a large living room near Brickerville in northern Lancaster County, Pennsylvania for our first Sunday morning celebration. DOVE Christian Fellowship International was birthed. (More details in the book: *House to House*).[1]

Our vision was simple: We were called to pray, make disciples and reach the lost for Jesus. This was done relationally through small home groups. One week I would preach the Word, and the next week,

I would serve in the children's ministry. We had our share of growing pains. Within the first six months, the original three small groups became two groups— we were multiplying backwards! But the Lord was so faithful to give us spiritual mentors who helped us to identify some of our mistakes and mature in our understanding of the basics of biblical leadership.

When our new church was about six months old, I met Ibrahim Omondi, a student from Kenya studying in the USA. We gathered with a few others for a prayer meeting in a barn near our home. God knit our hearts together and our relationship has now spanned more than thirty-four years. The many new DOVE churches planted in East Africa have been under Ibrahim's fatherly spiritual oversight.

During the first ten years of DOVE Christian Fellowship, our church grew to include more than 2,300 believers scattered throughout a seven-county region of Pennsylvania. We met in 130 small home groups during the week. On Sunday mornings, we met in larger clusters of congregations at eight different locations. We called these weekly gatherings celebrations.

In the mid-1980s, after moving our Sunday celebration from a house to a remodeled barn to a Christian school building and then to a renovated barn at Abundant Living Ministries near Brickerville, Pennsylvania, the building was filled to capacity. We started our second celebration, called the Southern Celebration, which met in the Sight and Sound Theatre near Strasburg, Pennsylvania. Eventually believers from this celebration planted churches in York and in Southern Lancaster County.

We sent a team to start a church in Wellington, Kansas and a church planting team to Central Scotland. We also started a Northern Celebration in Lebanon County that continued to plant new celebrations in Berks and Schuylkill Counties.

LaVerne and I led the Central Celebration at Abundant Living Ministries. After holding three services each Sunday, we eventually found a home at Westgate Auditorium in a strip mall near Ephrata. This celebration grew to 1,300 believers and soon teams were sent out to start new celebrations in Manheim, Elizabethtown, Ephrata and eastern Lancaster County.

Every few months believers from all the celebrations met together in a large auditorium or gymnasium or local park that we rented for the event. We turned over the hands-on leadership and ministry of the church to eight local church leaders and their leadership teams. Multiplying people and allowing them to move out on their own, affords limitless potential.

We also helped to plant churches in other nations including Scotland, Brazil, Kenya, New Zealand, Uganda, and Guatemala. Churches continued to birth churches. Some of these stories were told in this book.

Not all of these church plants continued on long term, and not all of these new churches stayed with the DOVE family, but there is such blessing in giving people an opportunity to plant a new church and spread the Gospel and build the kingdom. There is no failure as long as we keep our eyes on Jesus and on His kingdom and grow in the process.

Our focus was not on the large meetings. Instead, we focused on Jesus and on training believers to be leaders of small home fellowships. We realized that as people are trained, they should be released to start new churches.

An International Apostolic Council was formed to give spiritual oversight to this new apostolic movement we call DOVE International, and I was asked to serve as the international director. This "apostolic movement" was formed to become a family of churches with a common focus—a mandate from God to labor together to plant and establish churches throughout the world. We have found apostolic ministry provides a safe environment for partnering congregations and ministries to grow and reproduce themselves. On January 1, 1996, the one multi-site DOVE church in Pennsylvania took the step of faith to decentralize and release the eight local congregations to each become self-governing churches in the DOVE International family of churches. At the same time, DOVE churches in Kenya, Uganda and New Zealand also joined this new family of churches.

Since that time, we have had the joy of seeing dozens and dozens of churches planted and many others join the DOVE International family. Currently, about 300 cell-based congregations and house churches, and thousands of small groups from twenty nations serve with the DOVE International family. We are continuing to trust God for many more new small groups and churches to be started to reach a new generation of believers in Christ.

We are ordinary people who have made lots of mistakes and have stories that are not all success stories. But one key we have seen is the necessity of embracing the biblical truth of spiritual parenting. Each believer needs practical input from loving, seasoned spiritual fathers and mothers whose goal is to help them reach their full potential in Christ. Parents expect to see their children grow. During the past thirty-four years, it has been a privilege to watch many who were once "children" become spiritual parents and grandparents, as new believers, small groups and churches are added to our DOVE family. Read more about spiritual parenting in the book *The Cry for Spiritual Mothers and Fathers.*[2]

CHAPTER 23

Where do we go from here?

We have just read stories of churches being planted worldwide by ordinary people trusting in an extraordinary God. These are only a few of the many stories from the DOVE family that could be told about believers, just like you and me, who obeyed the call to plant a new church to reach more people for Christ. A thread found in every story is that the church planter took a step of faith. All of us felt insecure, often unprepared, and had to deal with the fear of the unknown, but each of us took a step of faith. Without faith it is impossible to please God. Our God rewards faith. What is God calling you to do? Is the Lord calling you to lead a team, to plant a new small group, a new church or to serve on a team with others who plant a new church?

Pluman and Mya and their adult daughter Lubrimyra live in Sofia, Bulgaria. A few years ago, they took a step of faith and obeyed the call to plant a new church in Sofia where Danail Tanev mentored them. They rented a building from another church in Sofia for the Sunday evening celebration meetings as believers in small cell groups come together each week.

Throughout the year, they led people to Christ who were not fitting into the church they had started in Sofia. In response, they wisely began new small groups becoming house churches for these new believers—new wineskins for the new wine.

Those who have told their stories in this book had to make a decision to become true disciples, not just converts. They had to deny themselves, and in their cases, this led to planting a church.

Jesus said it like this; "If anyone desires to come after Me, let him deny himself, and take up his cross, and follow Me. For whoever desires to save his life will lose it, but whoever loses his life for My sake will find it" (Matthew 16:24-25).

Recently I read Rick Joyner's *Word for the Week*, "A disciple lives a life of sacrifice, not pursuing our own desires, but denying them to take up our cross to follow Him who 'emptied Himself' of His divine nature to save us. Is our first response to seek our own desires or to deny ourselves for the sake of the Lord and His purposes? As He explains here, to live for ourselves is the path to losing our lives. Even the highest earthly goals bring only fleeting satisfaction and then emptiness. We were created for God's pleasure. Only a life devoted to this will ever fulfill us. To live the life of sacrifice we are called to is the path to the most fulfilling life of all."[1]

Obeying the Lord to plant new churches is choosing to live a life of sacrifice, but experiencing the fruit of our labor is so rewarding.

During the past few years, LaVerne and I have felt the Lord calling us back to our roots—helping to plant new churches in our own community. With some team members, we formed a new DOVE ministry called The New Initiative, which is focusing on planting new micro-churches in our community in Lancaster County, Pennsylvania. Two new house churches have already begun. These two new churches are committed to planting new churches. There will be many more God stories to tell in the coming months and years.

For those of you who sense God has called you to start a new church or to help start a new church, here are a few guidelines to help you:

1. Pray, pray and pray for direction from the Lord and for laborers for the harvest.

2. Focus on reaching new persons for Christ.

3. Disciple a new believer(s).

4. Help to lead a cell group.

5. Lead a cell group.

6. Multiply a cell group.

7. Discuss what you are sensing from the Lord with your church leadership.

8. Learn how to lead a Bible study (such as the Discovery Bible Study[2]), which takes people from not knowing God to falling in love with Jesus.

9. Meet with others who are called to plant new churches.

10. Receive training and take the DOVE Leadership & Ministry School either live or by streaming video anywhere in the world (http://www.dcfi.org/training).

11. Discern if you are called to lead a church planting team or if you are to be a part of a church planting team.

12. Discern the type of church you will help to plant: a community church or a house church. (Read the book *House Church Networks*[3] to know the difference).

13. Meet with others who have a heart to plant the type of church you feel called to plant.

14. Build a church planting team, or become a part of a team.

15. Develop a prayer base, a team of intercessors who will spiritually cover you.

16. Find ways to partner with others in this new vision.

17. Discern who will be your primary spiritual oversight connection when you plant this church.

18. Discern who will be possible mentors to you for this new endeavor.

19. Discern the Lord's timing with your team, spiritual overseers and mentors.

20. Pray, pray, pray and take a step of faith and expect the Lord to lead and bless you as you obey His call.

I have felt the Lord impressing me that He is giving us, the DOVE International family, an invitation. He says in His Word, "Ask me, and I will make the nations your inheritance, the ends of the earth your possession" (Psalm 2:8). I am convinced that God is inviting each of us to ask Him for laborers for His harvest, and to partner together with others to plant new churches in our communities, our regions, our nations and in the nations of the world.

Paul the apostle tells the Philippian believers, "In all my prayers for all of you, I always pray with joy because of your partnership in the gospel" (Phil. 1:4-5). This is how we feel about you. We desire to see you reach your full potential in Christ as we partner together to fulfill His purposes. As each of us do what our heavenly father asks of us, I believe our family of churches will grow to more than 1,000 churches by 2020. It is not about numbers, it is about responding to an invitation from our heavenly father to obey Him.

If you do not have a personal call from God to plant a church, ask God to help you find someone who has that call. Partner with them by praying, by helping them financially and by encouraging them. The person you partner with might live locally or somewhere in your nation or even in another part of the world. Develop a partnership with them and receive the blessing from the Lord as they plant new churches. Remember, Jesus said that when we give a prophet a cup of cold water, we will receive a reward like theirs (Matthew 10:41, 42).

The Bible tells us that without a vision the people perish (Proverbs 29:18). As we continue to grow as an international church family, we are called by God to fulfill the vision He has given us to build the church with an "underground" focus in the nations of the world. We are called to love Jesus, love His people and love the people in the broken world in which we live. And by the grace of God we will experience the daily reality of living the Kingdom—transforming our world from house to house, city to city and nation to nation.

2020 Challenge

An Invitation and Opportunity

*Ask me, and I will make the nations your inheritance,
the ends of the earth your possession.* Psalm 2:8

Slogan: People partnering to obey the great commission.

Mission Statement: Jesus has called us to obey the Great Commission by making disciples, reaching our communities and growing to at least 1,000 churches by 2020.

Churches will be planted in the following ways:
- Individuals planting churches
- Churches planting churches
- Partnerships for church planting

Partnerships are people working together.
This can happen:
- Locally
- Regionally
- Nationally
- Internationally

*In all my prayers for all of you, I always pray with
joy because of your partnership in the gospel.*
Philippians 1:4-5

Destination: 1,000 churches partnering to exalt Christ in many nations!

Sources

Introduction
1. Dr. C. Peter Wagner, *Strategies for Church Growth* (CA: Regal, 1987), 168.

2. Tim Keller, "Why Plant Churches" http://apostles-raleigh.org/wp-content/uploads/2012/08/Why_Plant_Churches-Keller.pdf

Chapter 1
1. Larry Kreider, *Biblical Foundation Series* (PA: House to House Publications, 1993)

Chapter 11
1. Brian Sauder and Larry Kreider, *Helping You Build Cell Churches* (PA: House to House Publications, 2004)

2. Larry Kreider, *Biblical Foundation Series* (PA: House to House Publications, 1993)

Chapter 16
1. Larry Kreider, *House to House* (PA: House to House Publications, 2014)

Chapter 18
1. Larry Kreider and Floyd McClung, *Starting a House Church* (CA: Regal, 2007)

Chapter 20
1. Larry Kreider, Ron Myer, Steve Prokopchak, Brian Sauder, *The Biblical Role of Elders for To-day's Church* (PA: House to House Publications, 2012)

2. Ron Myer, *Five-Fold Ministry Made Practical* (PA: House to House Publications, 2006)

Chapter 21
1. Mandate Discipleship School, Corvallis, Oregon. Website: www.themandate.info. Phone: 541. 224.7748

Chapter 22
1. Larry Kreider, *House to House* (PA: House to House Publications, 2014)

2. Larry Kreider, *The Cry for Spiritual Mothers and Fathers* (CA: Regal, 2014)

Chapter 23
1. Rick Joyner, Word for the Week (North Carolina: MorningStar, 2014) www.morningstarministries. org/resources/word-week/2014/defining-disci-pleship-great-commission-part-50

2. Discovery Bible Study website: http://worldmis-sionsevangelism.com/discovery-bible-studies/

3. Larry Kreider, *House Church Networks* (PA: House to House Publications, 2007)

DOVE Leadership and Ministry School can equip you and your team!

Many times this book mentions DOVE Leadership and Ministry School as quality preparation for church planting. Training takes place in the classroom or via the web and it's available to you!

Your church planting team can receive instruction at your church or home with live webcasts from DOVE-Hopewell School in Pennsylvania the second weekend of each month. Webcasting allows groups and individuals to attend DLMS remotely. Students send questions via text or email and the webcast chat feature allows for live interaction. Classes are available on demand for those with a time zone challenge.

For more about the school visit www.dcfi.org/training

MORE from LARRY KREIDER

Read Larry's blog at www.dcfi.org/blog
Like Larry and LaVerne Kreider on Facebook
Follow Larry Kreider on Twitter

House to House

How God called a small fellowship to become a house to house movement. DOVE
International has grown into a family of small
group-based churches and house churches
networking throughout the world. Includes
discussion questions. Use it as a handbook for
small group and house church dynamics as well
as a tool to train leaders. *by Larry Kreider,
264 pages:* **$15.99**

The Cry for Spiritual Mothers & Fathers

Returning to the biblical truth of spiritual parenting
so believers are not left fatherless and discon-
nected. How loving, seasoned spiritual fathers and
mothers help spiritual children reach their potential.
by Larry Kreider, 224 pages: **$14.99**

21 Tests of Effective Leadership

As leaders we all face tests. The greater our
call to leadership, the greater the tests will be.
Problems provide the opportunity for us to grow and
become more mature as leaders. No matter if we are
leaders in the workforce, in our homes, communities
or church, this book will help us stand when the task
becomes difficult. *by Larry Kreider, 218 pages:* **$16.99**

www.h2hp.com
Call 800.848.5892

Biblical Role of Elders
for Today's Church

New Testament leadership principles for equipping elders. How elders can be developed in today's church, what their qualifications and responsibilities are, how they are chosen, understanding fields of ministry, how elders are called to be armor bearers and spiritual fathers and mothers, how to resolve conflicts on eldership teams, and more. *by Larry Kreider, Ron Myer, Steve Prokopchak, and Brian Sauder, 274 pages:* **$12.99**

House Church Networks

A new model of church is emerging. Discover how these new house church networks offer community and simplicity, especially as they fit the heart, call and passion of the younger generations. These house church networks will work together with the more traditional community churches and mega-churches to show the transforming power of Christ to our neighborhoods. *by Larry Kreider, 118 pages.* **$9.99**

Cell Groups and House Churches

Are small groups new? This book provides a historical backdrop to much of what is happening in cell groups and house churches today. It points us to valuable lessons which the modern church can learn from history. Examine how cell groups and house churches developed in the centuries since the Reformation. *by Peter Bunton, 108 pages:* **$8.99**

www.h2hp.com
Call 800.848.5892